The Desert of Death on Three Wheels

Also by Antonio Graceffo

The Monk from Brooklyn: An American at the Shaolin Temple

Boats, Bikes, & Boxing Gloves: Adventure Writer in the Kingdom of Siam

The Desert of Death on Three Wheels

By Antonio Graceffo

GOM PRESS

An Imprint of Gom Publishing
Columbus, Ohio

PRESS

An imprint of Gom Publishing, LLC
P.O. Box 211110, Columbus, Ohio 43221

Phone: 866.466.2608
Email: communications@gompublishing.com
Internet: www.gompublishing.com

Library of Congress Cataloging-in-Publication Data

Graceffo, Antonio.
  The desert of death on three wheels / by Antonio Graceffo.
    p. cm.
  ISBN 1-932966-37-4 (pbk. : alk. paper)
  1. Graceffo, Antonio--Travel--China--Takla Makan Desert. [1. Takla Makan Desert (China)--Description and travel.] I. Title.
  DS793.T337G73 2005
  915.1'60459--dc22

                    2005013150

First Gom Press printing: June 2005

1 3 5 7 9 10 8 6 4 2

Cover design by Stephen Fox and Justin May

For all of those who came before me, and inspired me to follow:
Sven Hedin
Sir Richard Francis Burton
Bruce Chatwin
Marco Polo
Eric Newby
Peter Hopkirk
Sir Aurel Stein
Bill Whurst
Freya Stark
and Wilfred Thesiger, who once called Eric Newby a pansy.

Table of Contents

The Desert of Death
on
Three Wheels

1

In the rainforests of Central and South America, there is a species of frog, which comes in a variety of fluorescent colors – orange, yellow, red, and bright green. They are shinny and enticing, like living candy. The first thing you want to do when you see one is touch it. If you are a predator, the first thing you want to do is pop this exotic creature in your mouth. This species of frog bears the name *Poison Arrow Frog*, because its skin secrets a chemical so toxic, that the natives rub the edges of their weapons on it before setting out on the hunt. Touching this frog would be the last thing you would ever do. And yet, the desire is there.

A deadly thing can be compelling.

There is something relaxing about the slow, undulating sand dunes of the virgin desert. There is an untouched simplicity to that beauty which sooths the soul. In contrast to a desert landscape, the tropical jungles of South East Asia and Latin America seemed loud and pretentious, with their riotous explosions of florescent colors. Out here, deep browns and sandy yellows, slowly melted, give way to earthy reds and grays. It seemed somehow more honest.

On a clear day, nothing interrupts your view of the horizon, miles and miles away. It reminded me of my time as a merchant mariner, when on placid days at sea, I would seek out solitude by scaling the ship's one hundred foot smoke stacks. Something about the airy distance across the face of a gentle ocean would bring my mind and spirit back into alignment. The mountains and jungles never had this effect for me. But the desert was like an ocean. It healed me. And, I knew that I was one of the few Westerners to have ever experience the Taklamakan Desert so intimately.

Love often blinds us to the potential violence which lies beneath the thin veneer of beauty. That same ocean, which I found so therapeutic, nearly stole my life away on a violent night, when the ship became the plaything of waves, twenty feet high.

A storm on the ocean is a terrible thing. It plays on our deepest feelings of inadequacy and reminds us of just how small and insignificant we are compared to the ferocity of nature.

I would learn that the desert too had storms.

After hours of traveling at a snail's pace, I had given up on riding the bike. The wind was too fierce. Even standing up on the pedals, I could make no headway. So I limped along, dragging the useless hunk of metal behind me, like Jacob Marley, Scrooge's old partner, damned to dragging the weight of his sins chained to his body. I would have liked nothing better than to have just thrown the bike away. But that would have left me with no wheels. And I would surely have died of thirst before I could make it to the next oasis. The other thought which crossed my mind was to find shelter and wait out the storm. But this was out, because even sitting still I would need to drink ten to fourteen liters of water a day. The storm could last indefinitely. Glancing quickly at my reserve, I counted only five liters. I had no choice but to press on.

The Taklamakan Desert, also called *The Desert of Death*, is located in China's Xinjiang Province, formerly East Turkistan. It is the second largest desert on Earth. Scientists consider it to be the most dangerous desert in the world. But I am not sure how they measure these things. All deserts look pretty dangerous to me.

Traveling the Taklamakan Desert allowed me to

draw a line through item three of a list of about a hundred odd adventures that I hope to complete before starting a new list. I can't say there was much planning involved, however. It was one of my classic, spur of the moment decisions, made after months of wishing and dreaming.

The idea first came to me in December of 2003, while I was watching the TV channel sponsored by that magazine which ignores me. (That magazine which ignores me is my passive-aggressive way of referring to *National Geographic,* that has never responded to a single one of my queries.) The show was about three Americans who were so impressed with British explorer Wilfred Thesiger's crossing of the Open Quarter of the Sahara, that they quit their jobs, flew to Africa, and made an attempt themselves. Among his other major achievements, Thesiger is credited with being the first man, of any race, to cross the Open Quarter, a portion of the Sahara so desolate that even the Bedouins won't go there. He made the crossing three and a half times, as he was forced to retreat once.

Thesiger is also famous for having called British travel writer Eryc Newby a pansy. This fact, which Newby wrote about at length in one of his books, was considered to be so significant that it was mentioned in Thesiger's obituary. I don't know why I found this incidence so humorous, but I saved a collection of interviews, in which, over a period of years, each denigrated the other. It was the modern equivalent of Ernest Hemingway breaking F. Scott Fitzgerald's nose in a boxing match in Paris. Hemingway, like Thesiger, was a big bully. And, I don't think either of them would have tried such shenanigans with Alice B. Tolkas, Gertrude Stein's lover. She'd have kicked their ass.

The three Americans failed. But the trip was still significant, because it was the first attempt made on the Open Quarter since Thesiger, nearly fifty years earlier. Thesiger's desert adventures began nearly seventy years ago, so the Americans just assumed that he was dead. Imagine their surprise when they received a letter from him, not only verifying that he was very much alive but also inviting them to come meet with him in his home in the English countryside.

The meeting, captured on film by the magazine that ignores me, was touching. Thesiger, who had obviously grown more charitable in his old age, didn't care that they hadn't made it. He didn't call them pansies. To him, these men were heroes. The story actually brought a tear to my eye. I vowed, then and there, that I would have a similar adventure.

Africa was just too far away. I was very much embroiled in my Asian adventure, and was planning on leaving for the Shaolin Temple in March. I didn't want to interrupt these plans; neither did I want to put off the desert indefinitely. There are times we have epiphanies, and we feel like God has granted us some type of divine knowledge. There are other times that we have epiphanies, and we just feel like idiots for having missed the obvious. Thumbing through a copy of Rudyard Kippling's *Kim*, it occurred to me. Doesn't Asia also have deserts?

A quick check on the Internet verified a fact that most second graders knew, namely that there were in fact deserts in Asia. Since I wanted to keep with my Chinese language and culture studies, I looked for deserts in China. Again, I could have slapped my self when I discovered that the Gobi Desert, probably the second most famous desert, was located in China. But the Gobi Desert, for whatever reason, didn't sound remote enough or exotic enough to attract my attention. So, I kept searching. And that is when I found Sven Hedin.

Sven Hedin was a Swedish explorer in the early part of the 20th Century, who focused his exploration and writing on Central Asia. He was the last person ever to be knighted by the king of Sweden. His most notable achievement was that he was the first European to set foot in the Taklamakan Desert since the days of Marco Polo.

Now I was getting closer to home. Marco Polo was one of the names that every Italian American kid got crammed down his throat if he complained or gave up on anything. Polo, along with Enrico Fermi and Marconni, was one of our good guys, to counteract Al Capone and John Gotti, our bad guys. I know the adults were just trying to instill ethnic pride in us. But it was still damned annoying. In fourth grade, after two days of practice, I quit the football team and came home, only to be surrounded by scores of mustachioed relatives, both male and female, shouting at me. Would Marco Polo have quit? Would Joe DiMaggio have quit? Would Christopher Columbus have quit? Would Spiro Agnew have quit?

"He's Greek!" I protested.

Yes, and he quit. But no Italian would have quit. Rocky Marciano or Mario Cuomo certainly wouldn't have quit.

The other name that I recognized in connection with the Taklamakan Desert was the great Silk Road. Everyone studied that in school. The Silk Road runs right through Pakistan, heading east along the Karakorum Highway, and through the heart of the Taklamakan Desert.

Aside from the fact that it is the second largest desert in the world, how was it that I had never heard of it? And it wasn't just me. Probably seventy percent of the people who I talked to about the Taklamakan Desert had no clue. In fact, about half of them tried to convince me that I was mispronouncing Gobi Desert. But logic dictates that you would have to have a pretty advanced speech impediment to tongue-tie those two names.

The Taklamakan Desert, like many other adventure plans, slipped to the back of my mind when I left Taiwan to study at the Shaolin Temple in Henan, China. As much as the Shaolin experience was a non-stop, twenty-four hour a day occupation, there were moments of exhausted down time, when I lay on my bunk, and my thoughts turned to the adventure that the Taklamakan Desert surly held. At Shaolin, I felt the desert's pull perhaps more strongly, knowing that I was in the same country as this wild land of fantasy.

Eventually, I would have to escape the Shaolin Temple because of a nearly violent altercation with the Temple administration. I made it as far as Hong Kong, but because of the SARS epidemic, could not return to Taiwan. This left me with a lot of money in my pockets and a lot of free time in my second favorite city in the world. Just having been released from a monastery made my body hungry for much of what Hong Kong had to offer. And, fifteen months of being in the intellectual wasteland of Taiwan left my mind hungry for incredible titles that were available at the English language bookshops in Central District.

I loaded up on books about exploration and supplemented my reading with extensive Internet searches. The more research I did, the more the desert intrigued me. For one thing, although there were a number of famous explorations, most notably by Sir Aural Stein, up to the 1930s, there was precious little written about the desert in recent times. There was an account of an Italian woman in the 1990s named Carla Perotti, who made the first solo crossing of the desert. She dragged a custom built cart, which contained enough water for her twenty-four day odyssey. The only other recent exploration was a team, lead by Charles Blackmore, who made the first ever crossing of the desert from east to west. Even Sven Hedin had only crossed the short way, from north to south. Blackmore's route was several times longer. His book would become a kind of bible for me during my stay in Hong Kong.

I began contacting anyone who I thought could give me some guidance. The Royal Geographical Society of Hong Kong was extremely helpful, putting me in contact with a number of famous explorers. Although they were all friendly and offered what assistance they could, none of them had crossed the Taklamakan Desert. Finally, after weeks of searching, I discovered a two-paragraph story in a two-year-old edition of a college newspaper from the west coast of the US.

The brief narrative told of two friends, Alan and Bill, who had attempted to cross the desert but had to turn back when Bill was bitten by a tick and became life-threateningly ill. Further searches on the names of the two men lead me to their email addresses. Every phase of this research lead me closer to the opinion that the world of exploration was very small, and that the participants were extremely supportive and helpful to one another. Along these lines, Bill wound up becoming an excellent friend who has supported me and encouraged me in my life as a writer and an adventurer. At more than sixty years old, Bill still leads trekking expeditions on the glaciers of Pakistan. Once, we lost email contact for a period of months. Then, out of the blue, I received a message from him. *Sorry, I haven't written in so long, but I was on a Russian ice breaker, deep in the Arctic.*

When you tell people you are going to cross the Taklamakan Desert, the first words out of their mouth are *The what desert?* Once the geography of the desert is established, the next sentence is usually, *Don't do it. You'll die!* Even veteran explorers, like Charles Balckmore, were somewhat discouraging in their example. His crossing had taken three years of planning and cost half a million US dollars. Since my budget was zero, my experience the same, and my knowledge a little less, people were justified in telling me that I couldn't do it.

But Bill, and Bill alone, quoted the Nike commercial and said, "Just do it!" I asked him how long he and Allen had planned their trip. He said, "We didn't plan it." Bill and Allen had worked together on a boat in China. Bill had been ship's crew, and Allen was a lecturing Sinologist. Sometime later, Bill and Allen ran into each other in Hong Kong, where Allen announced his plan to cross the Taklamakan. Believing that Bill was the only one crazy enough to join him, Allen asked Bill to go. Bill agreed, and the rest was history.

"How much was your budget?" I asked.

"It cost US$1,200 for a camel and a guide."

"What equipment did you have to buy?"

"We bought a blanket and some vegetables at an oasis town, but the vegetables went bad after a few days," answered Bill.

"Carla had GPS and satellite phones and things. What did you have?"

"We had a compass, but it broke on the second day," said Bill.

I complained that I was unable to find reliable maps of the Xinjiang region.

"There are none," said Bill.

Not only were distances between towns and oasis different, or non-existent, on every map that I found, but also no two of them could agree on the names of the towns. One town, Kashgar, was also called Kashi, also spelled Kaxi, and at least two or three other spellings, so remote that I could barely recognize it as the same place. The capital of Xinjiang, Urumchi, was also spelled Urumqui and Urumulchi.

We even bought US Department of Defense satellite picture maps, and they were useless.

The discrepancy of names is partly explained by the fact that the Xinjiang region used to be an independent country, called *East Turkistan*. Throughout history, the country had, at times, been a loose collection of small kingdoms. And while the majority ethnic group was the Uyghur, a Turkic people who were a mix of Arabs and Turks, there were a number of other ethnic groups represented such as Kazak, Kiird, and even a small number of Tibetans and Mongolians. Each group had it's own language and writing system. So, many of the names I found were probably transliterations of the original names in a variety of minority languages. Later, as Uyghur, was accepted as the lingua franca among the minority people, the place names must have been changed to the Uyghur language. Since taking over the region in the early 1950s, the Chinese have renamed all of the towns, once again. So, some of the names I found were transliterations of the Chinese names.

In school we had learned, in geography class, that there were two types of barriers – natural and political. At times it is difficult to determine which is which. One explanation for the dearth of available information could be explained by the desert's remoteness. It is the point of the Earth which is furthest from the ocean. Another explanation would be that the desert now belonged to China. And that, more than any other factor, hindered exploration. China has historically been paranoid about protecting its borders. Most notably, China has always wanted a large buffer between itself and Russia. So, even in the days before the Communist revolution, Chinese policies about granting passports and permits for the desert were arbitrary and restrictive.

This prevented large numbers of foreigners from entering and exploring the desert. Historically, the Chinese themselves have never been great explorers. They even went as far as building a wall around their country, turning their attention inward rather than out. This left the desert virtually unexplored. During Mao's Cultural Revolution, fabulous libraries, museums, and monuments were destroyed. In fact, anything – human or otherwise – which could be connected to China's history, was done away with. During this time, many of the treasures, which the Chinese had not permitted Sir Aural Stein to remove from the country, were burned.

The Chinese concentrated much of their military forces in the Xinjiang region. This is, in part, a way to protect their borders. But it is also due to a separatist movement among the Uyghur people. There have been acts of defiance and terrorism in Xinjiang, directed at Chinese police and military. The Chinese have historically treated the region as an occupied zone, made wide sweeping arrests, and committed widespread violations of human rights. Since 1994, a Chinese policy of greater openness has slowly allowed foreigners some limited access to the desert. And international human rights groups began reporting on the violations committed against the Uyghur.

Since 9/11, George W. Bush accepted the Chinese government's claim that Al Qaeda fighters were recruited from among the Uyghur Muslims of Xinjiang. And that these fighters snuck over the border into Pakistan and then into Afghanistan, where they killed Americans, only to run back to China and disappear under cover, in Xinjiang. At the insistence of the Chinese government, George W. Bush allowed the Uyghur people to be added to list of the Axis of Evil. This has given the Chinese free reign to violate human rights. According to human rights groups, nearly two thousand Uyghur have been executed or disappeared since 9/11.

Part of the reason that I personally wanted to visit this region was for a kind of atonement. After 9/11 I had felt anger and hatred in my heart. I had even written a number of angry pieces, condemning Arabs and the religion of Islam. Now, with nearly two years of hindsight, I wanted to go to a Muslim land, meet the people, and learn that they were human – just like me. I wanted to see that they were no different from the people who died in 9/11, and that they had all the same fears, desires, joys, and pains as anyone else. In the desert, I met nothing but incredible hospitality and kind treatment. The Uyghur opened their hearts and their homes to me, and in spite of poverty and years of oppression, they shared with me the little that they possessed. Seeing the dignity and the triumph that they brought to their every day lives, I felt they were richer, in many ways, than I would ever be.

Bill explained to me that in the desert, there wasn't much in the way of navigation. Basically, maps and even compasses depended on having some stationary and permanent features to orient off of. In the desert there was nothing. You could navigate by dead reckoning, using the sun and stars, and do just as well.

In the end, it was Bill who convinced me that the crossing was not only possible but also could be done simply and cheaply.

My original plan had been to follow Sven Hedin's famous route, from north to south across the desert, from the oasis town of Hotan to the oasis town of Aksu. I scrapped this plan, in lieu of following the highway from Hotan to Aksu. This way, I probably wouldn't need a camel and guide. I also wouldn't need a compass. The only problem was how to carry water. But I figured that would sort itself out.

2

As an adventure writer, my work takes me to the remote and exotic places of the Earth. The trouble with remote and exotic places is that they are, by definition, hard to get to. And one can never know, in advance, what pitfalls may lie ahead to prevent you from attaining your goal.

On his first exploration into the Taklamakan Desert, Sven Hedin lost four of his men, eight camels, and four mules. One by one, they succumbed, in the grizzliest fashion, to heat exhaustion, thirst, dysentery, and hunger. Appropriately, The Taklamakan Desert has been called the Desert of Death.

Following in the tradition of my great hero, my first exploration into the Taklamakan Desert also nearly ended in disaster. It wasn't the fifty-mile-an-hour winds or forty-degree heat that nearly stymied my foray into the Desert of Death. It was my near inability to purchase a plane ticket that almost ended my career as an explorer.

My earliest attempts to actually book a flight and make arrangements for my Taklamakan Desert trip had been in Taiwan, a country plagued by the inability to accomplish anything. Information is impossible to get, even if you speak Chinese fluently, which I do. There are no yellow pages. And most businesses don't have web sites. Or, even if they have web sites, they don't own a computer, so they can never answer your email queries. The way you do research in Taiwan is that you ask your friend. He asks his friend. And, in theory, if your chain of friends is long enough, you can find out anything. In my case, however, this rarely works, because no one in Taiwan had even heard of the Taklamakan Desert, much less been there.

When the Taiwanese travel agent assured me that Thailand would be a more appropriate place to spend my vacation, I gave up and did what I always do when I get frustrated in Taiwan or when I need exotic products like maps or deodorant. I waited till I was in Hong Kong.

Hong Kong is a good city to use as a base for trips to China. It is easier to get around there. There is still freedom of the press. Information is readily available. And everyone speaks English. This last point, I would discover, was debatable. The truth about Hong Kong is that everyone is *supposed* to speak English. But the reality is that communication can be nearly impossible.

I walked into one of Hong Kong's largest travel agencies, took a number, and waited my turn. When the agent asked me my destination, I promptly told him.

"I want to go to the Taklamakan Desert, in China."

"Where?" he asked, baffled.

"The Taklamakan Desert."

"We don't have that listed as a travel destination," he said, glancing at his computer screen.

"No, you wouldn't. It's a desert. It is located in Xinjiang, if that helps."

"Where?"

"Xinjiang. You know – the Muslim Autonomous Region?"

"What country is that?"

"It's in China."

"Could you write it down for me?"

"Write what down for you? China?"

"No, Muslim."

I dutifully wrote out the word, *Muslim*, in block style, third grade print, but suspected that we were getting further away from my destination with every step.

"I checked the computer. There is no listing for Muslim. Are you sure that you spelled it correctly?" he said. He glanced at the long queue behind me, and I suspect he blamed me for holding up the line.

"Muslim is not a place," I corrected. "It's a religion."

"I'm sorry. There are no flights."

"Do you understand anything I am saying?"

My voice began to rise. Face it. I am from Brooklyn. I was screaming by this point.

"Perhaps there is a train," he suggested, confirming my suspicion that we were having a communication block. I speak fluent *Mandarin* Chinese, but the language of Hong Kong is *Cantonese*. Given the painful hours and months that it took me to learn Mandarin, I have trouble accepting the fact that there are some Chinese people I still can't communicate with.

"You are a Momo!" I told him. "Is there someone here who speaks English or Mandarin?"

"I speak English," he answered.

"No you don't."

He just gave a blank stare that said *This does not compute.*

Not knowing what else to do, I reduced the problem back to the original equation. "I want to go to the Taklamakan Desert, in China." This time around, I said each sentence once in English and once in Mandarin, to cover all bases. I even went as far as to write out the Chinese characters for Taklamakan Desert and Kashgar. I don't think that the average Westerner should be asked to do more than this when buying a plane ticket.

"I checked the computer. It's not in China."

"It was yesterday," I retorted. It really was. I had

even printed out a map from Mapquest. So, unless there had been a handover during the night, I had to believe that the Taklamakan Desert was still in China.

To prove his point, he showed me a map. With that look of *Aha! I have proved you are the murder!*, he triumphantly banged his finger on the map. That is not the Taklamakan desert. That is Tashkent. Tashkent was part of the Soviet Union. But I believe it is now one of the new Soviet Republics. Either way, it is neither a desert nor part of China. So, what part of *I want to go to the desert in China* made you show me that map? "

"Yes," he answered.

"Get me a Mandarin speaking agent now!" I was yelling again.

A woman, who looked infinitely more intelligent, walked over and introduced herself as the Mandarin-speaking agent.

We checked the computer. "Tashkent is not part of China," she confirmed.

"You needed a computer to tell you that? I don't want to go to Tashkent. I want to go to Kashgar, in the Taklamakan desert."

"Where is that?"

"It's above Tibet."

"Where?"

"Tibet?" I repeated in English and Mandarin. *Tibet, Shisan.*

"Oh, you want to go here?" she asked, handing me a map with a destination circled in green ink.

"Very good. Lahsa is the capital of Tibet," I said, reading the map. "But I don't want to go to Lahsa. I don't even want to go to Tibet."

"But you said Tibet."

"I said a lot of things. And you have chosen to ignore all of them. Why is this the one you have chosen to listen to?"

"You need special permission for Lahsa."

"No," I corrected. "I would need special permission if I were going to Lahsa. But I am not going to Lahsa. I am going to Kashgar."

"It's not in China."

"Yes, it is," I insisted.

"Where is it?"

"Taklamakan Desert. Have you heard of it? Second biggest desert in the world."

She just gave me the same blank stare that the first guy had given me. It must be something that they learned at travel agent school.

I gave her some more clues, in the hopes of jogging her memory. Desert? Samoa? No water? WHOOO Windy! WHOOO wind? No water? The second biggest goddam desert in the world?

Nothing.

"Do you know the Gobi Desert?" I asked, hopefully. "It's right next door."

"You want to go to Beijing?"

"Yes, I want to go to Beijing! I always say *Gobi Desert* and *Tibet* when I want to go to Beijing. That would explain why I have never been there," I said, sarcastically. "Look! I want to go to the second biggest damned desert in the world. It is one of only two deserts in China. So, just bring up a desert on your computer, any Chinese desert, and you will have a fifty-fifty chance of being right. The city on the edge of the desert is called *Kashgar*."

She typed away on her computer. "Oh, here it is. But you need a visa. And there is a war going on."

"NOT KASHMIR!" *You're all pigs and I'm ugly*! (This last part was only an internal monologue.)

I stormed out of the travel agent in a typical, Italian huff. As a result, I missed a very narrow visa window,

≡17

and my trip was postponed by two months. Sometimes, I think people from Brooklyn just shouldn't be allowed to live internationally. I don't know that we are the best cultural ambassadors.

From Hong Kong, I took a consulting job in Guangdong. Basically, the university I graduated from in England was forming a partnership in mainland China to open a series of schools and provide English teachers for Chinese public schools and universities. My first job was to do teaching demonstration and get schools interested in having certified teachers from Briton come and teach for them. The second part of my mission was to keep an eye on the local Chinese partner, read his documents, listen to his phone calls, ask a lot of questions, and find out if he was stealing from my employers.

It turned out that he was stealing from my employers. In fact, he had been ripping them off from day one. After submitting my final report, recommending that we not continue to work with him, he and I got into a shouting match, which ended with me hitting him. I only hit him once, but he smacked the ground hard, bounced, and rolled across the floor. Typically, this happened in a school, with about a million witnesses. Being one of only three foreigners living in the city, it was impossible for me to say, "It wasn't me." I barely made it to the ferry back to Hong Kong, a few steps ahead of the police. Unfortunately, I didn't manage to pick up my dry cleaning, and I lost two pair of custom made slacks. I also didn't manage to get all of the things from my apartment. So, I left my bicycle behind. It was one in a series of bicycles I would abandon in Asia.

Assuming that one of the things I had lost was my job, I decided to go to the Taklamakan Desert, information or no. This time, I found a better travel agent, one who could read a map.

Since I was now unemployed and on a very tight budget, I asked the travel agent for the cheapest solution. She told me that it would probably be cheapest to fly to the closest point in China, Guangjo, just over the border from Hong Kong, and then purchase an internal flight to the desert.

"How much would that cost?" I asked.

"I don't know. The Chinese don't make that information available. But we are sure it is cheaper."

"And when are the flights?"

"I don't know. The Chinese don't make that information available."

The Chinese were really opening up to foreign tourism, I thought.

The travel agent apologized for leaving so many of my questions unanswered. She explained that, since the Chinese did not publish their internal train and plane schedules, routes, or fares, the only information available to travel agents were reports from previous travelers. And, unfortunately, not many people had preceded me on this Taklamakan madness.

Since the Guangjo trip seemed too risky, I asked about other options.

"You could fly to Xian, in North Central China. From there, you could probably take a train," she said.

"And when is the train?" I asked. It just slipped out of my mouth, before I realized I had said it.

We laughed, and then both spoke at the same time. *The Chinese don't publish that information.*

The agent did some research and was able to come up with an even cheaper route. For just a few dollars, I took the train from Hong Kong, just over the border to Szen Zen. From Szen Zen, the flight to Xian was dramatically cheaper than it was to fly from Hong Kong. What's more, because Szen Zen was a special economic zone, fares and schedules were available. I was even able to purchase the ticket in Hong Kong.

I arrived in Xian in the early evening and asked the taxi to take me straight to the train station. The only view I got of Xian was out the window of my cab, but it looked much richer than Henan or Jiangmen, other places I had lived in China. Xian even had a Rolls Royce dealership. But I didn't buy one. I was beginning to believe the business theorists, who were now saying that there were small pockets of incredible wealth everywhere in China, and that any city, of any size, would be a good place to open a business.

As for the famed terra cotta warriors, I wrote a more detailed report for the State Department, but the gist of it is, I don't feel they pose a real, military threat. Although they are stunningly turned out, and stone cold disciplined, their apparent lack of weapons and opposable thumbs renders them virtually useless in combat. To further support my findings, I contacted seven of the major airlines, all of whom agreed that they would not be willing to accommodate passengers in excess of two thousand pounds, particularly not if they were unable to sit. So invasion by commercial jetliner would be out of the question. Once again, I believed the crisis was over. We could all rest easy.

I still didn't know where I was going. Assuming that the best place to start my adventure was Urumchi, the capital of Xinjiang province, where the desert is located, I tried buying a train ticket to Urumchi. But this proved a nightmare. The train stations in China were just the biggest, loudest, filthiest confusion of humanity on the planet. There were no signs in English or Chinese, and no one seemed to know anything.

There were long queues of people everywhere, like those reports we used to get from Russia, where people waited in line for days to buy bread. The queues snaked around the massive station, crisscrossing one another. I asked people what they were waiting for, but no one seemed to know. The Chinese are terrible at waiting anyway, but in a communist system, where the clerks are terrible about service, the whole station was just a huge pandemonium of people pushing, shoving, shouting. No one waited his turn in China. But maybe if he had waited, he wouldn't have gotten anything.

Every time I asked where to buy tickets, people pointed to the next building. I would fight my way into that building, and ask again. The answer was always the same. The next building. Even getting from building to building was nearly impossible because of the long queues. I kept thinking, if these aren't the queues to by tickets, then what are all these people waiting for? I never found out. The only information anyone was certain of was that it was illegal to bring a backpack into a train station.

In a country where everything was owned by the public, the baggage claim seemed to be a private enterprise, run by seedy people, of questionable appearance. Touts pounced on me, aggressively trying to convince me to pay them to check my baggage. But I refused. First of all, if I had checked it, I was certain that I would never have found that specific baggage claim again. Second of all, once they had my luggage, I could see them closing up shop and going home, maybe for a period of days, until I had given up on my bags and moved on. With the average monthly wage in China being less than the cost of a designer T-shirt in New York, or a decent pair of shoes in Taiwan, my backpack and its contents represented several years of income to anyone who could steal it.

In several instances the touts actually laid their hands on me, but I gave them a violent shove. At least twice a uniformed police officer said to me, "You can't come in here with that bag."

I smiled and, in a polite voice, said, "No, it's OK."

I guess I had the Jedi mind power on my side, because the cops just nodded sleepily and walked off.

Although I didn't have any negative experiences with police, it was still nerve wracking. Police were everywhere, eyeing you with suspicion. They frequently asked to see my passport, often asking me which of the English characters were my name. They wanted to check my visa, but couldn't read it. For whatever reason, while my entry visa was written numerically, my visa expiration date was written out, July 20. Since the police didn't know that July meant the seventh month, they just assumed I had an open visa and could remain as long as I liked. It was apparent that local police neither spoke English nor had any concept of dealing with foreigners. I guess they still had to check me, just to save face.

After several failed attempts, I found a line, which five out of nine people said was for the train to Urumchi. I tried waiting politely. But, as I said, this method didn't work in China. After twenty minutes we hadn't moved forward at all. Instead, I decided to use my ninety kilos of body weight to muscle my way to the front.

A ticket to Urumchi was only about three dollars. The good news was, the train was leaving in ten minutes. The bad news was, there were no seats left. So, I would be standing the whole way, thirty-six hours. It was either that, or wait several days for the next train. I would later learn that the third option would have been to pay a bribe of about US$5.00. But I had temporarily forgotten my bribe etiquette.

I wanted to buy a round-trip ticket, to save myself some trouble on the way back. But again, it just wasn't possible. You can't buy round trip tickets inside of China. I took the ticket and hustled through the crowd and confusion, looking for my train.

The train ride from Xian to Urumchi was a scene right from *Of Mice and Men*. I tagged along with two college students, who like some modern day hoboes, taught me how to ride the rails for cheap. Trains in China were not the luxurious affairs that they were in Briton or in Hong Kong. They were like everything else in China, devoid of any amenities, and designed to accommodate thousands of people. You could forget air conditioning or DVD movies.

The first seven minutes were interesting. It was the end of a school break, so I rode along with a ton of college students who were excited to meet their first foreigner. But, it didn't take long for the stuffy, crowded compartment to lose its charm. When the beer lady came around, I bought beer for all my new friends. I knew I needed to keep to my budget, but what was one thirty-second of a dollar between friends?

When I could keep awake no longer, I lay down on my backpack, right in the aisle, and slept. In China it is normal that people hock and spit constantly. Even worse, to kill time they often chew sunflower seeds, spitting the shells right on the ground. The floor was so dirty that I didn't want to get near it. But as fatigue wore me down, I wilted closer and closer, until I was wallowing in it. I was reminded of a recent travel book entitled *There is No Toilet Paper on the Road Not Taken*. Being an adventurer often means compromising one's standards of hygiene.

A lot of the people on the train were ethnic Uyghur, the Islamic, Turkic speaking people who live in Xinjiang. With each stop, the percentage of Uyghur increased. As people got on and off, they stepped over and on me, making for a horrible night. I had so many different shoe prints on my face and clothing, you would have thought that I had been kick boxing with Imelda Marcos. Combine my discomfort with my well-known aversion to travel and you'll understand why it is a good thing I couldn't speak the local language. I shouted the head off of anyone willing to listen, complaining about the trip. Luckily, the Uyghur didn't understand English or Italian, my swearing languages. They just smiled and gave me candies made from dried dates. They were good.

The next morning, at about 10:00 AM, someone found a seat for me. By 11:00 PM my neighbor departed, leaving me the whole seat for myself. I stretched out and got a little sleep. Unfortunately, I had been fighting a fever and diarrhea for over a week. Two sleepless nights on a train did me no good. I hoped walking five hundred kilometers in the desert would help me recuperate.

On the train I studied the little bit of information I had printed off the Internet and discussed my trip with people who lived in the desert. This gave me my first glimpse of what I was in for. Many of the Uyghur spoke no Mandarin at all. One of the ways that the Chinese government hoped to ensure their dominion over the region was by forcing ethnic Chinese to move there. As living in the middle of the second largest desert in the world is as much of a hardship as it sounds, the people who were sent there were generally people who broken the law or pissed off a party member. Often they were punished for sins committed by their parents of grandparents. I had heard of people being banished to the desert because their forbearers had been landlords before the Cultural Revolution. The most tragic story I heard was of a man sent by the government to study in Japan. When he returned, because he spoke Japanese fluently, he was considered a threat and shipped off to the desert.

In China, citizens are not free to move from place to place or even to change jobs, as we do in the West. If you were sent to Xinjiang, you would need a special permit just to go to your original home province, even for a visit.

Talking to the Chinese in Xinjiang, I didn't quite have the nerve to ask them what they had done to get sent there. They were my best hope at obtaining information, but they spoke an awful dialect that was very difficult for me to understand.

As foreigners were almost never seen there, people were always very curious about why I was traveling in such a remote area. A conversation I had with one woman on the train was typical of a dozen similar conversations I had during the long train ride.

"Why did you come here?" she asked.

"I am going to travel across the desert, probably by foot, from Aksu to Hotan."

"But why don't you go see the palace in Beijing? That would be a better vacation," she suggested.

"Because I want to see the desert."

"But why not take a bus? It would be much more comfortable and much faster."

"It's not about comfort and speed. I just want to cross the desert on my own power."

"The bus is air conditioned," she said.

"I'm sure it is. But that isn't what I want."

"But the desert is very hot."

Everyone sitting around us, who had been listening in, now agreed that the desert was indeed hot.

"Yes, I know. I watch National Geographic. But this is an adventure."

"It is very far."

"I know it is far."

"It won't be easy."

"Yes."

"Won't you get tired?"

"Of course."

"Then why do it?"

The idea of going into the desert, on purpose, was as foreign to these people as I was. They just couldn't get it. Another concept they didn't understand was going someplace, anyplace, alone.

"Where are your friends?"

"In Taiwan."

"Why aren't they on the train?"

"I am traveling alone."

"And your friends will meet you in Urumchi?"

"No."

"Well, how will your friends find you in the desert?"

"They won't. My friends are all back in Taiwan."

I think the listeners were more astounded that I would go on vacation alone than that I would risk my life in the desert, for no reason.

"Do you have a girlfriend?" she asked.

I had been living in Asia long enough to know that I could never answer *No* to that question. Somehow, Chinese found it inconceivable that I was unmarried. But that I didn't have a steady girlfriend was completely impossible to them. No amount of logic ever worked in these situations. Stating the obvious, *I can't get married or have a serious girlfriend because I am away from home nine months of the year*, did nothing to sway their opinion. So, I had long ago made up a girlfriend, named Linda, who I always talked about with great affection. I even carried photos of the two of us, which I showed to the train lady.

"But why didn't you bring your girlfriend with you?"

Did she miss the part of the story where I said I

was going into the Desert of Death? As tedious as this conversation was, the most disagreeable aspect was that I had to go through this exact set of programmed responses over and over again, until I returned to the civilized world of Hong Kong.

In Hong Kong, people understood. They said things like, *You are crazy! You will die!* But they always followed it up with, *I wish I could do something like that.*

The road not taken smells badly, I thought, returning to my seat from the restroom. The food on the train was cheap, but tasted horrible. For about twenty-five cents, you got a meal box with rice, a microscopic chunk of mystery meat, and a blob of smelly vegetables. No one seemed to know, or care, how long it would take to get to Urumchi. Even passengers going there gave me figures ranging from twenty hours to two days. Asking what time it was or what time we would arrive was also problematic, as there were two time systems in use. According to longitude, the hour in Xinjiang should have differed from Beijing. But because Beijing demanded that the whole country be standard, they imposed Beijing time on Xinjiang. The Uyghur, however, continued to use their local time. Train schedules were generally given in Beijing time. But asking anyone the time, you had to determine if he was ethnic Uyghur or ethnic Chinese, before adding or subtracting some hours.

How is it that the US doesn't feel threatened by our multiple time zones?

The landscape rolling past the train window was incredible. There were soft rolling mountains, which eventually gave way to step regions with low brush. Eventually, patches of desert began to pop up here and there. I saw my first dromedary camel, chained up outside a small shack, grazing in the sparse brown grass.

A college student was reading a book across the way from me. "What are you reading?" I asked.

"It is about Chairman Mao," she said, holding up the cover so I could see. "Do you know who that is?"

This was typical China. They just assumed that we had no idea about their country or their history.

" I know him. He's the money guy," I said, with a sly smile. (It rhymed in Chinese, *chien ren.*)

"The money guy?" they asked.

"Sure," I said. Fishing around in my pocket, I pulled out a 100 RMB note. "You see?" I said, matching the photo on the book to the man on the note. "It's him." Talk about a one-hero country. Mao is actually on all Chinese notes and all Chinese coins.

The kids laughed, although they probably weren't supposed to. At each stop a few of them got off. Before departing the train, each made a farewell speech to me, which reminded me of why I lived in Asia. The kids were just so well meaning and sweet. One of them even attempted to make his speech in English. No matter what hardships I had to endure in Asia, I didn't believe I would ever be able to go home again.

Although I was still uncertain of my route, the one certainty I had in my trip was that I wanted to pass through a large oasis town called *Kashgar*. During the heyday of British imperialism, Kashgar had played a pivotal roll in The Great Game, the struggle for domination in Asia, fought between Briton and Russia. Every traveler through the desert had to stop in Kashgar, and most notably at Chingi Ba, which was the British consulate run by Sir and Lady McCartney.

Chingi Ba had been a place where spies had passed messages, and where foreigners from all nations had celebrated Christmas and New Years. It was a place that played heavily in the literature about the desert. On the map, it appeared to be about half-way between

Aksu and Hotan. The problem was, I didn't know how far Aksu was from Hotan, or if I could make such a large distance before my visa expired.

Asking for information was impossible. No one, not even residents of Urumchi or Aksu could tell me how far it was to Kashgar. No one could tell me if there were towns in between Aksu, Kashgar, and Hotan. No one seemed to be able to tell me anything. Much of this was because people who lived in the desert didn't travel at all. The ones I saw on the train were probably people being granted their first leave in a period of years. Or they were students, returning from one or several years away at university. Again, this may have been their first trip out of the region.

People were giving me distances from Aksu to Hotan that varied from five hundred kilometers to two thousand kilometers. In the end, I decided that my best bet would be to get off at Urumchi and then buy a ticket to Aksu. In Urumchi I was hoping I could get some reliable information.

My first step out of the train station at Urumchi was easily as scary as Neil Armstrong's first step on the moon. I went from a Chinese train, a familiar scene to me, into this crazy street fair of Turkic people shouting and hawking goods in a language I had never heard before. The sights, the sounds, and the smells of the street in the Uyghur capital were reminiscent of anything but China. It could just as easily have been the bazaar at Marrakech, circa 1600. Any photos I took looked like they were taken in the Middle East. This was the most foreign place I had ever been.

Urumchi has been called the ugliest city in the world. It was certainly the ugliest city I had seen. Even Kemnitz, the eyesore of East Germany, had more aesthetic charm.

What was redeeming about Urumchi, of course,

was the unusual cultural mix. The Uyghur people made up about fifty percent of the population. All the street signs were written in Chinese and in Arabic script. Russians must also have been there at some time, because I occasionally saw signs written in Cyrillic. The Great Game continued.

There were mosques everywhere. To my untrained ear, the Uyghur language sounded exactly like Turkish. Many men wore skullcaps. Women wore headscarves. Occasionally, I saw women completely veiled like in more fundamentalist parts of Turkey or Arabic lands. A lot of the men wore a knife in a sheath on their belt. That really surprised me, especially in China, where I thought weapons were forbidden.

In a Uyghur restaurant, I had the best meal I had in weeks – roasted lamb and Turkish pizza! SOOO good! This was China? The meal cost 8.5 RMB (US$1.20). The set meal would have only been 6 RMB, but I ordered extra lamb and a specialty of Xinjiang, a big bowl full of chilled yogurt. That was my first yogurt since coming to Asia.

The appearance of the Uyghur people ranged from very Arabic looking, to almost Chinese, and occasionally very Western. There was an older man sitting across from me in the restaurant, wearing a type of beret common to Uyghur. He was built exactly like my father – short and wide, with the big shoulders and hands that come from a lifetime of hard work. His skin was the same color as my father's skin, about two shades darker than mine. His clothes were typical peasant clothes, worn by *contadini* from the Mediterranean to Russia. He looked like he could have been Corsican, Sicilian, Greek...anything, except Chinese. Which is what he was, and I could only imagine how he felt about that fact.

At first, I thought he was my father, and I asked for

some allowance. He refused so quickly that I was convinced he was my father. But then I remembered that Poppa doesn't speak Chinese. Maybe he learned Chinese to get off the allowance hook.

All the police, bus drivers, ticket agents...anyone with a civil service type job...was Han, ethnic Chinese. In spite of politics and racial inequality, I found myself gravitating toward the Chinese, since I could talk to them, and because they looked like everyone I had been living with for the last two years.

Buying train tickets was not for the meek in China. I fought in a scrum for thirty minutes, but finally had to give up and admit defeat. I walked out of the train station bruised, beaten, and ticketless. I checked into a hotel and slipped some cash to the concierge, who got me on an overnight train to Aksu. The trip would take over twenty hours, but I had a sleeper this time.

At every turn – getting on and off of trains, checking in and out of hotel – police and clerks always asked for ID. Since none of them spoke any English, I consistently used my Taiwanese identity card. When you change trains, you often have to go through a customs procedure like you would at an airport, filling in all sorts of nonsense forms. I wondered what these people would think if they knew that, not only could they drive from New York to California without being hassled, but also it would be illegal for the police to even ask them if they were foreign.

Since I couldn't read the forms myself, I just handed my Taiwanese ID card to the cops and asked them to fill them in for me. If you ever want to prove to the bureaucrats how stupid their bureaucracy is, sentence them to filling in their own forms. The cops usually got very annoyed and told me I had to fill it in myself. When they saw that I was incapable of complying, they would ask me to step out of line. This I refused to do, as I would have just been lost in the push of people, clambering for places on trains. In the end, the cops would begin filling in the form for me, generally get half way through it, and then just wave me through, shouting *Next*! They knew the forms were bull and yet they required them.

My question I, *in a country with a population of over a billion, who reads these forms? And where were they stored?* Judging by the poor quality of textbooks in schools in Guangdong, or the inexistence of textbooks in Henan, couldn't the forms budget be reallocated to the education sector?

The trip to Aksu was infinitely better than the trip to Urumchi. I slept much of the way and had a chance to do some reading. An old man in the sleeper below me asked if the long cylindrical object projecting from my backpack was a fishing rod. I had never heard the word before, in Chinese, and it took me a few minutes to understand what he was asking. When I showed him it was a kung fu fighting stick, he asked me do a demonstration. So, I stood in the tiny train compartment, swinging my weapon at various, imaginary opponents. Everyone clapped when I had finished. The only jacket I had brought with me on my trip was my uniform top, from the Shaolin Temple. I looked at myself as a cultural ambassador, transplanting Chinese culture to other parts of China.

This wasn't the last time someone asked me if I was on a fishing trip. I found this very strange, since, unless I had been horribly misinformed, there was no water in the desert.

3

Upon arrival, I checked into a hotel and went for a walk. This city was the last big town I would see in the desert. As my journey progressed, the population and character of the cities became distinctly more Uyghur. Now, Chinese people were clearly the minority. And Uyghur was the principle language spoken.

The architecture, however, was unmistakably Chinese Communist. Buildings were still made of concrete block construction. The streets were impossibly wide. There were very few cars, apart from an inordinate number of police and military vehicles. The most common conveyances were large tricycle rickshaws. There was even the occasional cart, drawn by a draft animal. As I strolled along the dusty streets, I was still uncertain of what form this trip would take. I had started with a vague premise of I will go to the Taklamakan desert and do something. The only other requirements were that I wanted to travel under my own power, and that I wanted to see Kashgar.

I was still having misgivings about even starting. First of all, I had thought the distance from Aksu to Hotan was only five hundred twenty-two kilometers. But a reliable source told me that this figure was the straight-line distance. In other words, it was only five hundred twenty-two kilometers if you crossed the heart of the desert, where there were no roads. Since I was following the road, the distance was going to be closer to one thousand kilometers. So, Hotan was out. I only wanted to go about five hundred or so kilometers. It turned out that Aksu to Kashgar was fine hundred forty-four kilometers. That was a distance that I could live with. So, now my trip was decided – Aksu to Kashgar.

The next questions which came up, were, if I were walking, how many miles could I walk in a day? How much water would I need in a day? How much water could I carry? How far was it between villages where I could buy water?

I had no answers for any of these questions. Arbitrarily, I decided to carry four day's worth of water. Sven Hedin had lived on four liters a day. So, that meant twenty liters. (I would later discover that I needed more than ten liters per day. But while I was safe in Aksu, I was still young and innocent.) At three pounds per liter, that was a lot of weight. I needed a better method than walking. Walking, I had set my odds at thirty percent.

While I wandered, I was pondering my dilemma, when I saw a seventy year-old taxi driver delivering four passengers to their destination with a *san lung che* (a tricycle rickshaw).

That was it! I could buy a *san lung che* and load it with four day's worth of water. I would still be within the rules of powering my journey with my own legs, and at the same time, I would be increasing the chances of both my success and my survival. With a rickshaw the bookies in Vegas had me at 3-to-1 against. That was still better than what I had me at, without one.

Everywhere I went in Aksu, people were staring at me. This wasn't necessarily a bad thing, as some of the Uyghur women were extremely beautiful. The girl who worked at the Internet shop, for example, sat with me the whole time I was doing email, chatting, and flirting. She told me that she was half Kazak and half Chinese. She spoke all three languages fluently – Chinese, Uyghur, and Kazak. She asked me my name, and I instantly replied, giving her my Chinese name, An Dong Ni. When I asked her, there was a long pause. Then she asked, "Do you want my Chinese, Kazak, or Uyghur name?"

"Chinese," I answered, because I knew I wouldn't be able to remember the others.

"Jiang Zao," she said, and it sounded like poetry.

She was studying English at the university, and had a Chinese boyfriend. But her mother would not let her marry the boyfriend because he was Buddhist, instead of Muslim. Jiang Zao was so charming, and so exotic, I actually considered hanging around town a few days to get to know her.

In a restaurant I saw three extremely fat women who looked like used up Russian prostitutes. I had met some like them in Guangdong, finding it appalling that Russia was now so much poorer than China that desperate women would come here to sell their bodies. Somehow, these Russians were never counted into the statistics as foreigners living in China. It was almost as if I were foreign, and they were just their own thing, existing in outer space.

Part of why people stared at me was probably because in their mind, there were only two races of people, Uyghur and Chinese. Since I was clearly not Chinese, I must be Uyghur. My skin is dark like theirs. I have facial hair. I must be Uyghur. They always spoke to me first in their language. When I told them, in Mandarin, that I didn't understand, they seemed offended. Later on, a wealthy Uyghur restaurant owner would tell me that the reason people were rude to me was because they thought I was a Uyghur, but I was wearing shorts. He said that if they had known that I was foreign, it would have been fine to wear shorts anywhere, except in a mosque. But for a Uyghur, even on the hottest day, wearing shorts was unthinkable.

While I was eating, a little Uyghur girl was looking at me, expectantly. Her parents kept encouraging her, saying things like, "Go ahead. Go ahead. Do it." Finally, the little girl got up her courage. She walked over to me and said, *"Ohio, dozai mask."* She was speaking Japanese! I had no idea where she had learned it. But these people had so little idea of where I was from, that they thought I was Japanese.

Before reaching my hotel, I witnessed one of those scenes that the Chinese government would probably prefer I had not witnessed. The streets suddenly filled with military and police vehicles. There were about twenty police, SWAT-style vans, countless patrol cars, and about a dozen People's Liberation Army deuce-and-a-half trucks, some of them with mounted machine guns. I had no idea how many people were involved in this action, but each deuce carried about thirty soldiers, armed to the teeth, wearing full flack-jackets, helmets, and face-shields. Each van had about twelve cops. All together, the figure probably approached six or seven hundred people, all waving automatic weapons.

The soldiers stormed an apartment house and came out seconds later with five Uyghur men, who they had already dressed in orange coveralls. The men were stood up in the back of the deuces. Their hands were cuffed behind their backs, and their heads were shoved through the railing on the side of the truck. The cops held the men by the hair of the head, so that everyone could see their faces. The vehicles got back in formation and made a slow parade through the streets of Aksu, almost like a warning to other suspected criminals.

During all of this, I had my camera in my hand, but was too shocked and, later, too frightened to make any photos. I was tense in my hotel room that night, afraid the police would come and question me about what I had seen. I would have used the Sergeant Schultz excuse from *Hogan's Heroes,* however – I see nothing. I hear nothing. I know nothing.

The next morning, I discovered, to my horror, that while paramilitary actions by police were part of the culture in Xinjiang, coffee was not. The hotel people directed me to one of two cafes in town, both of which charged 20 RMB per cup for this exotic drink. That was more than a day's salary for most people in rural China.

The highlight of my day was when I asked the desk clerk, "Where can I buy a rickshaw?"

"You want to hire a rickshaw? Why not just take a taxi?" she asked.

"No, I mean that I want to buy a rickshaw."

Disbelieving her ears, the clerk called for assistance. Chinese businesses usually have ten times as many employees as customers, and they all came running. It took some doing, but once I convinced them that I seriously wanted to buy a rickshaw, they scribbled an address for me. Unfortunately, most of the cab drivers couldn't read Chinese. My driver stopped passersby until he found someone willing to read the directions to him. We had to repeat this process several times before arriving at Rickshaws R Us.

In a developing Central Asian nation, the rickshaw salesman is the equivalent of the used car salesman back home. At first, he thought I was kidding when I asked to buy a rickshaw. In fact, he thought I was making fun of him. But after I assured him of my sincerity, he went right into salesman mode.

"This 'n here's a real beut," I imagined him saying in that stereotypical southern accent, which all used car salesmen had in American movies.

"Ain't got but two hunert miles on 'er. An them's

highway miles. Was took real good care of, too. Owned by a little ol' Uyghur lady who only drove it to Mosque on Sundays."

"You didn't turn back the odometer, did you?"

"Do what now?"

"How about that paint job? It looks awfully fresh. It isn't there to cover up body damage is it?"

"Friend, when you rode in here, you probably seen the name out front – Honest Omar. Now, Omar, that's me, an I'm here to treat ya right. Jus ain't no sense in taken folks fer they money. I'd rather sell a man three rickshaws in ten years then sell him one rickshaw in one year."

I tried to look unimpressed. That's what it said in the *AAA Rickshaw Buyer's Guide* on the Internet. You couldn't let the salesman feel he was making any headway with you, or the price could skyrocket from US$35 to US$40. Also, the book warned, not to fall for their charm or their false flattery. The book actually said, "Used Rickshaw salesmen are better than Chairman Mao himself at winning over the hearts and minds of the people."

"Of course, a smart feller like you probably do better with a camel," he suggested.

"Well, I wouldn't go so far as to say that I was smart, maybe a little well read," I said, nearly succumbing to his charms. But then I saw through his cleverly disguised ruse. He was doing what the book called a*dd ons* – getting you to pay for all of those little extras that you originally had no intention of buying, such as livestock or beasts of burden.

"NO!" I said, putting my foot down. "No camel. I came here to buy a rickshaw, and I'm not leaving till you have sold me one."

"Alright. I can see yer a man who knows his stuff. It's a shame about the camel, though. I got one in this morning consignment from a feller who's fallen on hard times. It seems his best mating rooster died, killed tragically in a cock fight, and now he needs to *unload*, I mean *sell*, this camel in a hurry, or his whole coop of chickens is gonna' die out. He said he'd let it go for a song."

"A song, huh?" Once again, I almost fell for the old bait-and-switch, where they lure you in by showing you the price tag on a used rickshaw, but then talk you into buying a fully loaded, brand new rickshaw, or in this case, a camel. But I made it clear that I was only in the market for a basic, used rickshaw.

"How much was you plannin' ta spend?"

"A little less than standard price," I answered.

"What kind of rickshaw was you wantin' ?"

Not being very experienced in buying rickshaws, I gave him the one criterion I insisted upon.

"Give me a red one."

I also had a choice between large and small. But since at this point I still wasn't sure if I was just playing an elaborate practical joke, I bought the smallest one they had. This way, if I got two miles out of town and quit, I wouldn't be out so much money. It was hilarious seeing this two hundred pound foreigner with a New York Yankees cap trying to ride a tiny three-wheeled cycle with a Barbie doll camper in the back. I suspect that he sold me the one rickshaw he had been trying to sell for months, but couldn't find a big enough sucker to take it off his hands. As I made my uncertain way down the street, bouncing off of stationary objects like a drunken racket ball, I saw the other shop owners come over to congratulate Omar on his sale.

There would be much rejoicing at the Omar house that night.

Apparently, riding a rickshaw was nothing like riding a bike, because I absolutely couldn't control it. I kept running into things and bouncing off of walls. When I finally said, "I'll take it," the man asked me where I was headed.

"Kashgar," I answered.

He laughed. "But you can't even ride out of my shop. How are you going to ride to Kashgar?"

I admitted that he had a point. But I figured that by the end of five hundred forty kilometers, I would be an expert.

After a frightening trip to the grocery store, where I was all over the road like the Captain of the Exxon Valdese, I loaded up the rickshaw with food, water, and my gear.

The rickshaw, with three spare tires and a pump, had cost me 330 RMB, or a little less than US$40.00. The people at the hotel, however, were convinced that I had been over charged. I had no point of reference. The way I saw it, if this trip worked, I was going to get ten days of adventure, followed by an excellent story, for less than the price of a dinner out in New York.

When I tried to checkout of the hotel, there was a huge problem, because I didn't have my receipt to prove that I had checked in.

"Since I am handing you the key, I think it is safe to assume that I had indeed checked in," I pointed out.

"But you have no receipt. How do we know it is the same person?" said the clerk, sounding like a suspicious customs agent in a spy thriller.

"Because I am the only foreigner in the hotel, possibly in Aksu. And, furthermore, you are the one who checked me in."

"I'm sorry. I cannot allow you to check out," said the clerk, gravely.

"What do you mean I can't check out? Are you saying if I leave the key on the counter you won't pick it up? Or are you saying that you will prevent me from walking out the door?"

"These are the regulations," she said, avoiding my question.

This is what I loved about China. Everything was regulated. Every action required fifty permits and a hundred signatures. The government controlled everything, and yet nothing worked.

In the end, the hotel manager intervened. "I will only do this for you this one time," she said, handing me a new receipt. "Next time you stay, here I won't be able to help you."

"OK, next time I am in Aksu I will remember that," I promised.

The nice thing about China is that they never want anyone to lose face. So, any momentary lapses of manners are always followed by moments of smiles and good cheer. The whole hotel staff came out to see me off and to get a look at my crazy vehicle. They were all laughing and smiling, but still suggested, "Wouldn't you be more comfortable riding the bus to Kashgar? That way you wouldn't be tired when you get there."

They just didn't get it.

I made it about three blocks, when I realized I didn't know how to get to Kashgar. So I rode back and asked directions. A truck driver wrote out a map on the back of a cocktail napkin. And off I went.

I rode down the streets of Aksu, very dangerously and badly, singing the *san lung che* song that we had learned at the Taipei Language Academy. *San lung che poude quai. sha mien zwo lau tai tai...* I couldn't get the stupid tune out of my head. I kept wishing Clapton had written a rickshaw song that I could sing instead.

The only people who drove rickshaws in Aksu were Uyghur. So people stared and stared. I also hadn't shaved in a week, and I had a good tan. Basically, I think everyone thought I was a Uyghur. They all tried talking to me in Uyghur language. I got very rude treatment from a number of them when I answered in Chinese. In one instance, a group of men actually looked like they wanted to throw hands with me.

Just outside of town, the road surface was all broken. The ride was bumpy and unpleasant. The problem with the rickshaw was that it was not a bicycle. It was designed to carry heavy loads, across short distances, inside of cities. If you tried to climb up hill, the chain just slipped off of the rings. If you tried to go down hill, it would go completely out of control. Like a van or a jeep, the rickshaw had a tendency to flip over pretty easily. It steered somewhere between a truck and a boat. When you wanted to turn, you just turned the handlebar ever so slightly and waited for the bike to come around. Any sharp movement on the handlebars would spill you.

If the bike got away from me, there was no stopping it. My body, plus my gear, plus the bike probably had a combined weight of three hundred pounds. The break was a huge lever, halfway down the frame, like on a buckboard wagon from *Little House on the Prairie*. It was not designed to control the speed while riding. It was really just a parking brake. When the bike would get out of control, taking my hand off the handlebars to operate the break lever was one of the most counter-intuitive things to do.

Riding the bike was a real upper body workout, because you had to pull hard on the handlebars, against your pedaling and the bike's tendency to turn right. This actually proved a better workout program than living in the Shaolin Temple.

On a flat, even road surface, it was fairly pleasant to tool along, at a snail's pace, sitting upright, and taking in the sights. The first two days there was actually a bit of vegetation to look at. I didn't enter the full-blown desert proper until the third day. I felt like I was drifting along, like Huck and Jim, floating down a slow, hot, Chinese river, made of black tar. The weather wasn't too bad. Yes, it was hot – very hot. But it was a dry heat. I always laughed at people who used that expression in the past. It's forty-five degrees Celsius, but it is a dry heat. But it really is true. Desert heat was not as uncomfortable or as debilitating as moist tropical heat, like in Guangdong or in Taiwan.

Temperature and weather were two more facts, like distances, that I just couldn't verify before going out there. All of the reports I had read said that the temperature in the desert ranged from a high of forty-five during the day to *minus* forty-five at night. Somehow, I just couldn't believe that those measurements were taken on the same day. Still, I kept reading that at night it would be very cold in the desert. Once again, there was no specific information given. The reports just said very cold. Was that cold relative to forty-five degrees Celsius? Or was that cold relative to the freezing point of water? I didn't know. Consequently, I packed way too much clothing.

The first two nights, when I wasn't quite in the desert proper, the temperature at night felt as if it dropped to, or slightly below, room temperature. It was probably about twenty-four, or even twenty-two degrees. On those nights I had to wear a sweatshirt to bed. But once I was in the desert proper, it was so hot, even at night, that I slept in just my shorts, or as little as possible. On the periphery of the desert, there were problems with mosquitoes. So you had to cover up at night. But in the desert proper, there was almost no life of any kind. So you could sleep with your skin exposed to the cool night breeze.

In Aksu I was unable to by large bottles of water, so

I was carrying a crate of twenty-four 600 ml bottles. I drank one every forty-five minutes, and restocked my supply every time I came to a village. Since dehydration is the major killer in the desert, I was careful to check my sweat and urine. If you stop sweating, this means you are in serious trouble. You could potentially be suffering from heat stroke and could easily slip into a coma. In a tropical climate, you drip sweat. I found that in the desert, although I was sweating, it evaporated quickly. If I went jogging in Hong Kong, I could take off my shirt and ring water out of it. But riding a bicycle all day, if I stopped for two minutes, my shirt dried out. One way I knew that gallons of sweat were evaporating through me, however, was that there were tremendous salt stains on my clothing. It was like when you had been swimming in the ocean and then sat out in the sun to dry. You would actually be able to scrape the salt off of your skin.

In the military we had been taught to check our urine when working in a hot weather environment. Basically, the closer it is to clear, the safer you are. This means that there is a high percentage of water in your urine. Too high is not a problem. (Yes, it is possible to die of drinking too much water, but it is extremely unlikely. In the world, somewhere on the order of three people die per year of over hydration. Whereas thousands will die or suffer severe effects from dehydration.) If your urine begins to change color, you need more water. Yellow means that you need to drink water. Brown or red mean that you are in a dire situation. If you stop urinating, this is very dangerous. It means that your kidneys have shut down. The rule of thumb, which we were taught in the Army, was that you should drink at least one quart of water per hour, and you should be urinating once per hour.

Any time I noticed discoloration, I stopped wherever I was, sat down, and drank two 600 ml bottles of water. My capacity for water in the desert amazed me. At home, I don't think I could just sit down and drink that quantity of water. But in the desert, I drank three or even four of those bottles at a sitting. I couldn't imagine how Charles Blackmore's group made it through on four liters per day.

My clothing consisted of my New York Yankee baseball cap, military shorts, hiking boots, and a cut off t-shirt. I used sun block forty-five and glacier strength lip balm. The only medicine I carried in my pack was Imodium, aspirin, disinfectant, and bandages.

The bike had exactly one, very slow, optimum speed. Any attempt to go faster simply caused the chain to slip. And you could forget about standing up on the pedals. That would end in disaster, as you would slip the chain and flip the bike. Every time the chain slipped, my knee swung around and collided with the sharp edge of the break lever. This happened several hundred times a day, making me look like the head nurse from that old joke.

I cursed myself for not having any duct tape to wrap the brake lever in. I hadn't bought any in Aksu. In fact, the list of equipment that I didn't buy was rather extensive. This was mainly because I didn't think I would make it this far. This far being out of Aksu.

The road ended at the entrance ramp to the Karakorum highway. This ramp almost proved to be my Waterloo. There was a constant flow of construction vehicles up and down the steep ramp. On a regular bike, I would have geared down, stood up on the pedals, and shot ahead of them. But on this crazy three-wheeler, riding was out of the question. Even walking, the grade was too steep for me to push the bike up the hill. Meanwhile, at every attempt, I was taking my life in my hands as cars were bearing down on me from both sides. The plan had been foolish and ill conceived from the beginning. At this point I actually thought it might make more sense to cut my losses, turn around, and go home.

Just then, three Uyghur construction workers were walking up the ramp. As soon as they saw me, they ran over and helped me push my bike to the top. There was a lot of laughing and smiling between us. It seemed that this rickshaw really endeared me to the Uyghur since, in a way, this was their vehicle. This would not be the last time that Uyghur workers would stop to help me with my bike.

Shortly after turning onto the main Karakorum Highway, I saw a sign which read *Kashgar 440 km.* I would not see another sign for Kashgar until I saw one which said *Kashgar 42 km.*

I stopped at a Uyghur restaurant and ate a huge meal of goat meat and excellent Uyghur bread. At this stage there were still a few Chinese restaurants. They would be the last I would see until I arrived in Kashgar. There were cars coming in and out of Aksu. By the end of the second day, the only cars I would see would be the long military convoys and the endless legions of trucks, trading with Pakistan. At least twice on that first day, Chinese people stopped their cars to get out and chat with me. They asked me about my trip, gave me some water, and then requested that we make a photo together.

I had gotten off to such a late start, that by eight o'clock in the evening, I had only been going for four-and-a-half hours. I needed to get out of the sun, which was still high. But in the desert, there was no shade at all. There wasn't even anything that cast a shadow. As there was still a bit of vegetation this close to Aksu, there was a tree line, about three hundred meters from the road. I doubted that the short, scrubby trees would afford me much protection from the sun. And, it was too far to take my bike. Neither did I want to leave my bike by the side of the road.

I saw a power pole with a brick base. The base was one meter wide by one-and-a-half meters high. If I lay on the ground and curled up in a fetal position, the shadow just about covered my body. I stayed like that till sundown. I had a long wait. No one had mentioned this in their books or articles, but the sun didn't set until about 11:00. As the sun oozed around to the west, the shadow would shift position, and I would move with it. By nightfall, I was 180 degrees away from were I had started. I think there was a lesson in astronomy there, but I was too depleted to know what it was.

While I was resting, I needed to eat and drink water, but to do that I would have to stand up and brave the sun. Tentatively, I reached a hand out to my backpack, but jerked it back the second the sun's cruel rays struck it. I felt like Bella Lugosi, awaiting the night, when I would be able to roam freely. For dinner I ate some Uyghur rice, which was left over from my lunch. I also had flat, round Uyghur bread, huge Uyghur bagels, and some dried Uyghur sausage.

I drank countless 600 ml bottles of water and spent my first night on the ground beside the highway. I didn't have a tent or a blanket. But it wasn't very cold, so this was no problem. What was a problem, however, was that I was eaten alive by mosquitoes like nothing I had ever seen. I sprayed half a bottle of insect repellent (Deep Woods Off) on my body, but the mosquitoes just laughed at me. They covered every inch of my exposed skin. At one point, I glanced down at my hands, and they were black with the bloodsucking bugs. I put on my long pants and jacket, wrapped a t-shirt around my face and head, and slept fitfully. Around two hours after sundown the temperature dropped again, and the mosquitoes abated a bit. I took the t-shirt off my head and stared up at the night sky. It was huge. There were no mountains, no buildings, and no clouds to obstruct this perfect, heavenly view. The stars shone like spotlights.

As far as I knew, I had made it about twenty-five kilometers that first day. That wasn't bad, considering how late I had started. I still wasn't mentally committed to making it all the way to Kashgar, however. Anyone could do one hard day of cycling. But to get up and do it again, the next day, and the next, for ten days, that was a different story. In the back of my mind was still the possibility that I would quit, abandon the bike, and hitch a ride into town.

4

In the morning, I woke up after sunrise, and went through a morning routine of washing, brushing my teeth, and putting in my contacts. I tried to use my contacts the whole trip because it would have been very painful to travel during the day without sunglasses. My breakfast consisted of Uyghur bread and sausage, and tons of water. I would have loved some coffee and a shower. But I would get neither for the next week.

I passed by a strange looking mosque which was surrounded by, what I took to be, small stupas. The place had an eerie feeling about it. I suspected it was a graveyard, and the stupas were actually mausoleums. I pulled off the road to investigate, and was met by an ancient Uyghur man. He was wearing traditional Arab dress of floor length robes and was wearing a skullcap. His gray beard grew down to his belly. He looked to be about seven hundred years old. I gave him the local greeting, *Asa lama Alichum.* Then asked in Chinese if I could make some photos. He babbled on and on in what I presume was Uyghur. I, of course, couldn't understand a word. I held up the camera and pointed to the stupas, as if to ask if I could make a photo. The man kept babbling on energetically. He also blocked my way, making it clear that I wasn't to enter the little compound. He reached out and touched my beard a number of times, for some strange reason. What struck me was that he didn't seem to show any recognition toward my camera. Perhaps it was the first time he had ever seen one.

Trying to make him understand that I had come a long way, I held up the American flag that had been tied on my backpack since 9-11. If he didn't recognize my camera, he definitely didn't recognize the flag. I was astounded. Someone who didn't recognize the American flag? How could that be? I told him in Chinese and English that I was American. But he didn't get it. Taking a bottle of water from my bike, I offered it to him. Even this sealed plastic bottle seemed to be an unfathomable mystery for him. He placed the bottle back on my cycle. Next, he started picking through my clothing and things. If he had wanted something that I could spare, I was willing to give it to him. He may have thought I was a traveling salesman. In the end, he just shooed me away, and I didn't get any photos.

When I thought about it later, I guess it wasn't that strange that he didn't speak Chinese. Why should he have? He was already old when East Turkistan became part of China. And why should he have heard of America or known about cameras and plastic water bottles? These weren't part of his reality. I didn't see any family around. Perhaps was a hermit. He probably lived as he always had, with the cares of the greater world far, far away.

It was strange that he hadn't heard of the New York Yankees, however. OK, he never saw an American flag. But he never heard of Yankees baseball? What kind of backward culture was this?

The day was awesome. I got the hang of riding the bike, and rarely went off the embankments or ran into cars. There was a river running beside the road, across from a construction site. I was just debating whether or not to go skinny-dipping when the construction foreman came over and addressed me in Uyghur. I asked him to repeat in Chinese and was surprised to hear him speaking the same Henan dialect spoken at the Shaolin Temple. I showed him my Temple jacket, and we talked about my stay there.

The foreman invited me to eat with them. Lunch would be at 1:00. Until then, he had a seventeen year old boy, one of the young workers, lead me back to the camp so I could take a nap in their big, communal tent. The boy told me that all of the workers were from Henan. He said that he missed home a lot, and that it was his dream to study at the Shaolin Temple. Once again I had that feeling of privilege. I had come all the way from Brooklyn to study at the Shaolin Temple. He probably lived down the street from it, and could only dream of studying there. The tuition, for Chinese students, was only 300 RMB per month. I almost offered to pay the fee for him. But God knew why he was out there in that wasteland. I wondered if he was helping his family by contributing his earnings. Or, had he screwed up, and he was being punished? Or, had his father screwed up, and so the family was being punished?

The rest did me good. Lunch was a big bowl of smelly Henan noodles and filthy vegetables. I was only able to eat half of mine. The young boy ate the rest for me. It is always embarrassing, but because I am the guest, and because I am so much bigger, Chinese hosts always load me down with food. But I just can't eat that much in one sitting, even if the food is good. And, in China, the food is usually not good.

After eating, we all slept a few more hours. Afterwards, the foreman and some of the workers called me to join them sitting in the shade, and I told them about my insane trip. The workers told me that they napped from one until five every day to beat the heat, and suggested I adopt the same schedule. The men were all from Henan, and it was nice to hear the language we had spoken at the Shaolin Temple. I told them about the temple, and they told me about their lives, so far from home. They had to live at the construction sight, from April till November. Then they could go home. They worked seven days a week, from 6:00 AM to 1:00 PM and then from 5:00 PM to 10:00 PM – or later.

The foreman asked me how much my boots cost.

They had cost me about US$60 dollars. "720 RMB," I said, converting the currency.

He shook his head and laughed. "I earn 500 RMB per month. Your boots cost more than my monthly salary."

Next, he asked me if it was true that all Americans were rich. I told him that it wasn't. But everything about me told him that we were rich. First of all, he would work seven days a week, probably without any vacation, for the rest of his life. And he had probably been doing that since he was fifteen, or even younger. He knew that I, on the other hand, could take off from my job for months at a time, to study at the Shaolin Temple, or to travel in the desert.

In spite of good intentions, at every step, I drove the point home to him.

"How much is a plane ticket to the US?" he asked.

"About one thousand US," I said.

Not only the quantity of money suggested wealth, but even the fact that I had just assumed that he would know the conversion rate to US dollars. He just stared at me blankly, but knowing that I was used to dealing with Taiwanese and Hong Kong Chinese, who he also assumed were very rich.

"How much is that?" he asked.

"12,000 RMB," I said.

I hated myself for answering his question. But, I couldn't lie. And I couldn't claim that I didn't know. Of course, now I had confirmed for him that my plane ticket had cost more than a year-and-a-half of his salary.

"Foreigners are all rich," he concluded, shaking his head. All the other workers agreed. "How much could I earn in America?" he asked. The others all sat up on their heels eager for an answer. Looking into those work worn, weary faces, it was clear that they wanted to hear the tales of gold on the street.

I imagined that during the siesta, after a hard morning of picking olives back in Sicily, my grandfather and his friends had gathered around the one *contandine* (peasant) who had a cousin in America and asked the same question. The cousin was, most likely, much poorer than he had been in the Old Country. Even worse, he was desperately lonely, because he had left all of his family and friends behind. But, in order to save face, he only sent rosy letters home, which told about how he had become wealthy in the land of promises and dreams. Believing those tales, the desperate poor of Europe made an exodus to America. Some became wealthy. And some didn't. But for most, this old Italian saying was the truth:

"I came to America because I heard the streets were paved with gold. When I came to America, I discovered that the streets weren't paved at all. And, they wanted me to pave them."

Not wanting to perpetuate these types of myths, I almost answered his question truthfully. How much could you make in America, with no English and no high school? The same as you make here. Instead, I tried to explain, which was the wrong thing to do.

"In a city like New York, working in McDonalds, you would probably earn about US$800 – roughly 10,000 RMB – per month.

"Waaaa!" they all exclaimed. Now that they were hanging on my every word, I hoped to lay this issue to rest, once and for all.

"But an apartment in New York would cost you

$1,500 per month. So you see? Your salary would only cover half your rent. And we haven't even begun to discuss the cost of food, electricity, clothing, or transportation."

"EIGHT HUNDRED per month! Americans are rich," they all agreed. Once again, I felt like a moron. The fact that they missed the point, and the fact that I had expected them to get the point, said a lot about both of us. I had no clue about the realities that faced them every day. And, they had no clue about the realities that would be facing them in ten years, as China entered the market economy.

Already, I had read a statistic that China had more millionaires than the US. At the same time, wages in China were nearly the lowest in Southeast Asia. Special economic zones were popping up all over the country. There was a huge push to teach English in schools. In Guangdong, it was actually illegal to speak Cantonese in a school building. There were signs everywhere, which read *Please speak Mandarin or English.*

While people in the West marveled at Chinese whiz kids, mathematics champions, and concert virtuosos, education was largely unavailable to the average Chinese. Mandatory education was only for nine years. And China still lagged the West by a significant margin on the percentage of kids who would go on to higher education. The difference in wealth and education between the urban areas and the countryside was growing steadily. I personally met schoolteachers in Henan who only possessed a high school diploma. They taught in one-room schoolhouses where fifty kids, ranging in age from about six to nineteen, studied without books, paper, or pencils.

How could I expect these men to understand the concept of cost of living to wages ratio? How could China expect these men to make the jump into the new century? I guess the answer was that China didn't expect them to make it. That's why they were in the middle of the Taklamakan Desert doing construction work.

The boy asked me how long I was staying. I thought he meant, how long I was staying in China. I said, "I will stay until I reach Kashgar. Then I will fly back to Hong Kong."

He shook his head. "No," he said. "I mean how long are you staying with us?"

I laughed. "Just a few more minutes, then I have to get on the road."

"But why don't you stay a few days?" he asked.

"I can't. I have to move on."

Actually, it wasn't like I was on a schedule. I guess I could have stayed. Anyway, the boy was very cute in his innocence and his persistence.

The boy looked very sad.

"You should stay a few days," said the foreman. But then, catching himself, he restated, "The boy really wants you to stay. And I don't mind."

I had to laugh. This was the hold that Asia had on me. Would this have happened in the US? Well, we don't really have Gulag-style work camps like this one. But if we did, would they have invited me to stay on?

"Thank you for being so kind," I said. "I wish there were something I could do for you."

The foreman's countenance changed, and I could see his next question was difficult for him. "There is something you could do," he said, as if he was certain I would refuse. "Could I see your passport?"

It sounded a little strange, but I handed it to him. He took the document on the palms of both of his outstretched arms, as if it were a gift from the Pope. He turned it over, magically in his hands, afraid to open it. I lifted the cover and showed him the inside.

The picture seemed to take him by surprise. Finally, he handed it back to me.

"I have never seen a passport," he said. And by this, I knew that he meant he hadn't even seen his own passport. Chinese citizens are not in physical possession of their passport. What's more, they have to apply for an exit visa if they want to leave the country. It is generally not granted. (Although, now there are special arrangements being made for business men, in the major cities, as well as citizens living in the five special economic zones. But as a rule, the vast majority of Chinese would never be permitted to leave.)

"America is far away," he said, in awe.

The Chinese are such nice people. Only their government is insane. I always felt bad for my Chinese friends. They just want what everyone wants, the right to come and go as they please. How is it that Europeans and North Americans are allowed in and out, and yet our countries are not collapsing into ruin as a result? But yet, China is afraid to let people out.

"You Americans have independence," he said. The word he used was not *du li*, meaning an independent nation. He said *se yo*, which is more personal. It has more of a meaning of self-reliant.

"We Chinese are not," he added, sadly.

As much as I love China, it is an emotional roller coaster. Why wasn't this nice young boy in school, dating cheerleaders, and playing sports with other kids his own age? And why wasn't this foreman allowed to go visit other countries? And who thought it was a good idea to separate these men from their families for month at a time? And what did any of this have to do with communism versus capitalism?

These types of conversations were ones I had had at the Shaolin Temple. The food was exactly like Shaolin – extremely bad, dirty, and with that Henan flavor. The familiar food and language, combined with the communal living and sleeping arrangements really took me back to the Temple. I missed that lifestyle.

Eventually, against their protests, I convinced them that I had to go. The boy led me to the road and nearly cried as I drove away.

I hit a number of difficult gradients, where the road surface was broken, and I used a lot of energy pushing my bicycle. At one point a truck stopped in front of me, and a Chinese politician got out, shook my hand, gave me water, and made a photo with me. He offered me a ride, but I turned him down. He reached behind the seat and handed me a melon. Xinjiang is famous for their melons, and this gesture would be repeated time and time again. I sat right on the side of the road and ate the whole melon with my pocketknife. It was heaven.

About an hour later, I came on a small town, the first one I had seen since Aksu. Everyone in this village seemed to be Uyghur. In every town I visited in the desert, the restaurants were set on a shaded veranda, in front of the owner's house. In addition to the tables and chairs, they always had a bed where you could catch a nap. I stopped in a restaurant to buy water, and some Uyghur truckers called me over to their table. Truckers tended to speak pretty good Mandarin, so we sat, drinking tea and chatting. While I was there, I decided to eat lunch. There was no menu. I simply said, "I would like to eat." The owner came back a few minutes later and gave me a huge plate of goat meat, Uyghur bread, and soup. It was absolutely delicious.

On the way out of town, old men sitting on verandas along the road called me over to drink tea. But I just smiled, shook my head, and shouted, "I am going to Kashgar."

Outside of town another truck stopped and gave

me water.

At around 7:15, I decided to stop for the night. Once again there was the problem of where to find shade. All day I had been noticing that both the highway, and the railroad which paralleled it, had these large drainage tunnels dug underneath. They tended to be about five feet high, eight feet wide, and twenty feet long. They were cool and clean inside. Basically, they made a perfect home away from home for me. I unloaded my bicycle, carried my things down the embankment, and put them in the tunnel. Then I went back up, got my bicycle, carried it down, and set it out in front of my cave where I could keep an eye on it.

I was feeling a little bit sick and depleted that night. I also felt lonely. The only real conversation I had had in the last several days had been with the construction crew. I didn't sleep exceptionally well in the desert. Sleeping in these drainage tunnels, which I did for the rest of the trip, was better than sleeping out in the open, but it was still a little spooky being out in the desert alone. I kept thinking maybe someone had seen me and was just waiting for me to fall asleep, so they could come kill me and rob me. They probably could have left the body right there in the tunnel, and it would never have been found. Each night, I slept with my kung fu fighting stick in my hand. Every time I heard the slightest noise, which was *always*, I would pop up in a stance, wielding my weapon.

On the map there was a town called *Bachu* (not the capital of Azerbaijan), which looked to be about half way between Aksu and Kashgar. Unfortunately, after carefully examining the map, which sucked, and after talking to the truckers, I got the impression that Bachu might actually be a full day's ride off of the highway. That would mean a day out, a day back, and I would still be no closer to Kashgar. I decided to scrap my plan of catching a shower and getting a good night's sleep in Bachu.

I was still traveling without any information at all. Someone had told me that Kashgar was still nine hundred kilometers away. Since I had originally thought it was five hundred kilometers, and I had ridden for two days, this really surprised me.

The construction guys had asked me, "What are you planning on doing in Kashgar?"

"I don't know," I said. I hadn't thought about it. "Turn around and go home, I guess."

The truck drivers had asked me where I had come from.

"Aksu," I said.

"Why were you in Aksu?" they asked.

It was pretty much the same answer: "I don't know."

I guess that they couldn't accept the concept of traveling for traveling's sake.

The specific verbiage that the woman on the train had used was *Why don't you bring your friends here to play?*

I wished I had given her the answer that was in my mind now, after two days of hard cycling in brutal heat. First of all, I don't consider saddle sores and sunstroke playing. Second of all, not all of my friends want to take time off of work, go to China, and travel through a desert.

I slept much better in my cave than I had anticipated. The mosquitoes were much less of a problem than on the previous night. Things were a bit quieter, as well. Plus, I think there is just a certain security to having two walls and a roof around you. At first, I had tried sleeping width-ways in the cave, but a rodent ran over my legs, scaring the daylights out of me. So, I switched around and slept lengthwise. That way I wouldn't be

=59

blocking the vermin traffic lanes.

5

Going was hard in the morning. My butt ached as if I had been the victim of a wild Saturday night in a prison. My extremities were coated with a thick film of sunscreen, salt, sand, and dead bugs. The sunscreen was a bit sticky, so every time I swatted a bug the carcass remained glued to me, like bugs on a windshield.

I hit a village early in the morning. It reminded me of the Uyghur equivalent of deliverance country. The people all looked very strange, and conspiratorial, as if I had just interrupted them slaughtering the last bicycle tourist in the basement. An old woman in a black dress stood out on the road, selling water from the top of an overturned wooden crate. There was an old man on a tractor who didn't take his eyes off me. He got down from the tractor, picked up a fence post, which I had no trouble imagining he could use as a weapon, and remounted his noisy steed. While the woman fumbled for change in a box behind her makeshift counter, the old man drove the slow moving beast onto the road and began making for us.

It was Sunny Corleon all over again. Someone, probably the Solatso brothers, paid off the woman to drop the change, and then while I waited for it, this old guy was going to turn me into mulch with his tractor. They'd split up my Jimmy Buffet CD collection between them, and then let the kids dance on my guts till I started to smell. I may have been a little paranoid from all the heat, but I didn't like that tractor sneaking up on me. Instead of waiting for change, I grabbed two more bottle of water, thanked the crazy lady, and took off. The man on the tractor looked disappointed.

The children ran after me with stones, but they didn't throw them.

Unfortunately, that was the last village I saw that day. After that, I made it my policy to buy water at every single opportunity. I would drink my fill while standing at the water sellers. Then I would refill my thirty-six-bottle crate and buy as many other loose bottles as I could stuff around my bike, usually about eight more. Once I left that village, I was in the desert proper.

Now there was no vegetation at all. But, the landscape was still beautiful, or even more so. Off to the left was a low mountain range, which would follow me almost all the way to Kashgar. There was no shade, no dwellings, and no place to buy water, as far as the eye could see. Although I had such a large supply of water, I felt a little panicky. Being out in the desert alone is very much like being out on the ocean in a lifeboat. The distances seem so vast, and you feel so small and helpless. To make matters worse, my tiny bicycle was impossibly slow. On these flat open places, I could be doing fifteen kilometers per hour, or better, on a racing bicycle. Instead, I was probably doing about six kilometers an hour on my clown bike.

Speed is essential in desert travel. On a racing bicycle, moving three times as fast, you would have had three days worth of water and food purchase opportunities every day. This would dramatically increase your chances of survival.

I had to take a lot of ass breaks at this point. My butt hurt like no pain I had ever felt. For the last hour or so, I had been looking for a place to eat lunch and get out of the sun. My first choice was a Uyghur village with a restaurant. But scanning the horizon, it didn't look like that was very likely to happen. With my slow bicycle and the open road, I could probably see two hours riding distance into the horizon. Eventually, I became so exhausted that I gave up on finding a village and would have settled for another railway tunnel where I could curl up in the shade, drink some water, and eat some of the food from my pack. Unfortunately, the railroad veered away from the road, and it was just too far to carry my bike, probably about two kilometers.

Eventually, the railroad veered again, and came within five hundred meters of the road. It was still too far to carry my bicycle, across the parched and broken earth, but I desperately needed a break. I manhandled the bike down the embankment and dragged it across the ground, which looked like the surface of the moon. When I could drag the bike no longer, I simply left it. I walked to the drainage tunnel, taking what I needed to relax – food and water, a book about General Stillwell in China, the Rent sound track, my Billy Joel collection, and my Walkman. I was still a little nervous about the bike getting stolen, but realistically, I didn't think anyone would stop their car, run out into the desert for two hundred meters, steal my bike, and drive off with it.

One of the Uyghur breads I was eating was a tremendous bagel. The New York Times ran a story, once, on the origin of the bagel. Some said it came from New York. Others said it came from Israel. The Times said that it was a bakery product created by Jews in Poland. I beg to differ. I can't imagine that there was so much cultural exchange between the Uyghur and the Poles. So, my guess is that they came from here, or from the Turkic peoples of Central Asia.

During these rest stops, I would alternately eat, drink, sleep, listen to music, read, and write in my diary. Some of the writing was strange, stream of consciousness stuff.

Diary, 07/20/2003

I discovered some cavities in my left rear molars. It has been four years since I have been to the dentist. The camel is the ship of the desert. Bullshit! My bicycle is the ship of the desert. My bicycle looks so hot and lonely out there in the sun. The wind blowing off the desert into my cave is hot. I think I made the right choice to rest. All of my injuries are aching. I guess at thirty-six you just don't heal anymore. Left hand, right wrist, and right knee all painful. The hand was broken fighting at Shaolin. I can't quite straighten it out now. The right hand was sprained boxing in Jiangmen. The knee was screwed up doing kung fu in Taiwan. Who says exercise is good for you? The knee is holding up. But it is swollen and doesn't want to bend when I walk. Somehow, constantly pushing the pedals doesn't bother it. But running, jumping, and kicking are all a problem. I miss my friends. April is facing a horrible dilemma. Probably won't have Internet until Kashi. Family will probably be worried. I wonder what Miao Hai is doing.

I stayed in the cave until after 4:00 PM. During that time, I drank eight bottles of water. When I immerged, I felt much better. A few miles down the road, Uyghur man, standing in the middle of nowhere, selling melons from the back of his horse-drawn wagon. I stopped to eat one, only 4 RMB, and he even cut it up for me. A while later, I found a Uyghur restaurant and had my daily, Fred Flintstone-sized portion of goat's meat. For the second time on the whole trip, I found a sign. It said, 343 km to Kashi.

My camp that night sucked. I couldn't find a cave, so I slept out in the open. I was deeper in the desert now, and the sand was fine, like powder, invading every orifice of my body. It was extremely hot, but the bugs were a problem. So, I still had to wear everything I owned.

After that, I always slept in drainage tunnels under the highway or under the railroad. I also took my noon rest there. It kept me out of the sun and away from prying eyes. I generally slept uneasily, though, a little afraid of intruders. I kept my kung fu fighting stick at my side all night.

By the morning of the third day, I was certain that I was going to make it. By that I meant certain that I wasn't going to quit. I could still get killed or have an accident, but now I knew I wasn't joking. I already began planning how I would tell the story, in Forest Gump fashion, when I got back to Hong Kong.

I would say, "I rode my bicycle across the Taklamakan Desert."

They would say, "So, you just rode?"

"Yup. I rode to the edge of Aksu. When I got there, that felt pretty good. So, I thought I'd ride into the desert. When I got there, that felt pretty good. So, I thought I would ride all the way to Kashgar. When I was hungry, I ate. When I was tired, I slept. And when I had to go, well, you know, I went."

At ten o'clock at night I could still see to write in my diary. I sat at the edge of the drainage tunnel, reflecting on the trip. Although the temperature dropped at night, holding my hand three feet away from the bricks, I could feel the heat radiating out. Now, when the Uyghur rode by, they were wearing their evening clothes, jackets with very long robes. I was still wearing shorts. While we may suffer in extreme heat or cold, I think people from temperate climates are the

=65

most adaptable. Here, a drop of a few degrees sends the locals running for cover. Taiwan was the same way. Normal room temperature was twenty-six degrees. If the temperature dropped to twenty-four or, God forbid, twenty-two, the Taiwanese put on every scrap of clothing they owned.

Luckily there were no mosquitoes. There were, however, a few flies. I was a little bit worried about scorpions and snakes. But hadn't seen any. The ground was cracked and barren, covered with a thin layer of crust. When you stepped on it, the crust instantly gave way, and you sank up to your ankles in the powdery sand. As slow as my progress has been on the road, sixty kilometers per day, Blackmore and other who had gone through the interior of the desert, walking on sand even less stable than this, averaged less than twenty kilometers per day. There were days when the progress was in single digits.

Now the desert was truly remote. I only saw one truck pass every half hour or so. Across the open expanse you could hear an approaching vehicles for miles and miles. The headlights were also visible long before the vehicle arrived. During the night I heard a repetitive clopping sound. It was a slow, even, rhythmic stomping, coming from somewhere in the dark, beyond my vision. I held my flashlight in one hand and my fighting stick in the other. As the noise approached, I imagined some hideous beast which grew larger and more hideous with each passing second.

"It's nothing," I said, trying to convince myself. "When it arrives, you will see that it is nothing, and you will have a good laugh at yourself." But it wouldn't arrive. I waited and waited, the noise continued, and yet I could see nothing. I forced my eyes to pierce the distance. There was nothing there that I could see. The noise became louder. It must have been only a few hundred meters away. Then, I caught a flash of something, some suspicious movement. It wasn't a man. Neither was it a car. There was something floating in the air, and below it a faint light flashed. Now I heard voices.

Not until the object was nearly on top of my position did I realize that it was a horse drawn wagon, driven by two Uyghur. The men appeared to be floating, because the wagon's dark color made it virtually invisible. The flashing lights I had seen was the moonlight, playing on the spokes of the wheels as they went round. It was nothing. The Uyghur were as startled to find a large white man, naked, except for his underwear and a New York Yankee cap, swinging a fighting stick, out in the desert, alone, at night.

I made up a riddle. *What has four arms, eight legs, and clops?*

Answer: *Two Uyghur on a horse drawn wagon.*

Admittedly, it wasn't a great riddle. And the places that people would understand it were limited. But it did add local color. I promised myself, that if I published any writing about the desert, I would probably delete the riddle from the story.

It was so hot in this part of the desert, or maybe it was just that my body was overheated. I was laying out in just a pair of under-shorts, trying to cool off. Chinese workers, like the ones I ate lunch with a few days ago, were very casual about dress. Around their camps they tended to strip down to shorts, covering up only when they went back out in the sun. But the Uyghur wore layers of clothing, including a jacket and two shirts all the time. It seemed funny to be modest in these climes, but I was afraid I would offend some nomad, who just happened along, materializing out of the dark. When the headlights came, I would cover up, nervously, and not breath easily again until the truck had passed. Unfortunately, it took about fifteen minutes from the time the headlights of a truck became visible to the time its taillights had disappeared.

My saddle sores were so bad I could only sleep on my left side. My *pigu* (Chinese for behind) hurt like the time Sister Rosa beat me with a yardstick for putting drops of water on the eyes of her glow-in-the-dark statue of the Virgin Mother, and claimed I had witnessed a miracle. Now, just like then, it was hard, even painful, trying to sleep on only one side. Tossing and turning was excruciating. It didn't help matters that my accommodation was one of the worst of the whole trip. The tunnel was nearly filled with gravel, which bit into the open sores on my flesh. I found myself uttering sentences that would have made no sense anywhere else. I wish I had the cave where I took my nap this afternoon. Now that was a cave to be proud of!

When I was in the Merchant Marines, ship assignment was by the luck of the draw. Sometimes you got a good one. Sometimes you got a bad one. And no matter how satisfied or dissatisfied you were on a given ship, there were always guys on the same crew who told about ships they had served on which were better. A shipmate of mine once said, "There are only two good ships in the merchant marines: your last one and your next one."

Maybe this was true of these drainage tunnels, too. Tomorrow, I would surely find a better one.

The next day, a man stopped his car to chat with me. He was also kind enough to use my camera and make a photo of me. The difficulty with being on these trips alone was that there weren't many photos of me. Most of he Uyghur, while well meaning, couldn't – or were afraid – to use the camera. Also, their Chinese was often so limited that I couldn't explain to them what they needed to do.

The life up here seemed to be very hard. I have written about the villages on the roads, where I bought water. But many Uyghur lived in even smaller villages, sometimes collections of six or seven dwellings, several hundred meters from the road. Just as a cultural experience, I considered visiting one of these villages to see how they lived and if they even had restaurants. But, it would have meant abandoning my bike and walking across the crusty surface of the moon.

In the settlements where I bought water, Uyghur made their living with small restaurants, tiny bicycle and auto repair shops, and small grocery stores. Out here, there were a number of Uyghur selling melons. But the principle occupation seemed to be herding goats. In fact, other than beasts of burden, predominantly horses, the only other animals I saw in any great numbers, were goats. The young boys herded the goats back and forth across the desert all day. It seemed an exercise in futility, as I couldn't imagine the grazing being better in one part of the desert, where there was no vegetation, than in another part of the desert, where there was no vegetation.

While I was in Hong Kong dreaming about this trip, I had considered living up here for a period of six months or so and learning the language. I have always had a strange desire to learn at least one extremely obscure, nearly useless, form of communication. If the Uyghur were shocked when I spoke Chinese, imagine how blown away they would be if I spoke Uyghur. But now I was rethinking this. For one, while the desert is beautiful, people just don't look that good up here. Even with all of the precautions they took, their skin still turned to leather. People I had talked to, who looked to be in their thirties, often told me that they were in their late teens. Living here for that length of time would be an aesthetic six months.

One guy, at nineteen, looked to be at least ten years older than me. He was married and had two kids. Not only did this seem too young for us, in the West, but it was actually against Chinese law. In China, men are not allowed to marry until twenty-five. In keeping with the general hardship and unappealing appearance of the desert dwellers, I hadn't bathed all week, and yet I didn't feel embarrassed when I was eating in restaurants or talking to people. I suspect that even the people living in the villages didn't bath. Workers out in the desert certainly didn't.

My general rule was, I didn't want to live in a place where smelling as badly as I did, I could still get the best seat in a restaurant.

Some people looked a bit stunted, both physically and mentally. I wondered if this was the product of living in a desert, where there wasn't a lot of opportunity for sports or intellectual development. Or, was this the result of inbreeding? As I said, many of these villages were tiny. When I would ask how far to the next village, people often didn't know. This told me that they may never have been to the next village. If they were only marrying within their village of seven families, it wouldn't take long for the gene pool to become homogeneous.

On a separate note, I was disappointed that the only camel I had seen so far was tied up to someone's front porch. It wasn't even a camel which was indigenous to the region. In one of the books I read, I discovered that, although camels occur here naturally, they are endangered. So, many camels have to be imported from the Middle East. It seemed a little artificial to me.

In a restaurant, the guy asked me how much meat I wanted. I wasn't sure what the units were, so I picked an arbitrary number. Five. He reached into an ice boxed, which looked to be only marginally cooler than the prevailing air temperature, and removed three quarters of a goat carcass. He took up a big cleaver and brought it down on the carcass five times. Each time, it fell with a resounding *thunk*! The five huge hunks of meat, bone, and gristle were tossed into a pot of greasy water, which contained the remains of all the other meals he had cocked that day, and maybe of the previous day as well. When the meat turned a sickly gray he fished it out of the water, dropped it in a bowl, and served it to me with a loaf of bread. A vegetarian would die in the desert.

Barbaric? Yes. Filthy? But of course. Tasted great? Absolutely. Now, while I sit in an apartment in Taiwan and type these pages, my mouth is beginning to water, as I remember those incredible meals that I ate in the Taklamakan Desert.

In the movie Casablanca, The German SS officer Major Strasse asked Humphrey Bogart's character, Rick, "Why did you come to Casablanca?" Bogart replies, "For the waters." The Major looks suspicious. "But Casablanca is in the desert. There are no waters." Rick answers, "I was misinformed."

If I were to be arrested by the PLA (People's Liberation Army) and asked why I had come to Xinjiang, I would answer, "For the meat." And there would be no way anyone could disagree with me.

I kept thinking about the tiny portions of goat's meat, rotating slowly on a spit at a Turkish restaurant back in New York. For that infinitesimal quantity of meat, they charged US$8.00. My dinner the previous day had only cost 6 RMB (50 cents US). On this day it was 30 RMB (US$2.25). When I protested, the restaurant guy claimed that this was because I had eaten five pieces of meat, at 5 RMB each. Even though I was being ripped off, the same meal with that quantity of goat's meat, would have cost US$40.00 back home. And this is just theory, as most likely no one had ever eaten a meal with that quantity of goat's meat in a restaurant in New York.

That night I found a very comfortable cave, and slept well. The next morning, I felt rested but was plagued by diarrhea. By late afternoon, I had taken five Imodium, but was still having problems. In the desert, diarrhea could be lethal, because it caused your body to lose water. My stomach was severely cramped. This, combined with my saddle sores, made ridding painful. I walked the bike most of the day. From one o'clock to five o'clock, I rested in a very comfortable cave.

When I emerged from the cave, the afternoon heat was horrid. During the whole of the day, I only came across one Uyghur drink stand.

That night, I slept under the railroad, where the drainage ditches were infinitely more comfortable than the ones under the highway. They were much taller. So, I could stand up; no stooping. They were also more private as they were further from the road. I derived a kind of security from the fact that I could watch the road approaches from my railroad cave. But when I was sleeping under the road, I couldn't see who was coming and going above me. Perhaps Robin Leech, from *Life Styles of the Rich and Famous*, should do a show, comparing the life of the sub-railroad dweller to that of the sub-highway dweller. In describing the advantages of the railroad cave, he would definitely use the adjective *commodious*. I loved that word, and would have liked to use it, but it seemed too pretentious coming from me.

By the time I camped for the night, my stomach had recovered fully. It was now so hot that the second I got out of the sun, I took off everything but my under shorts, and drank four liters of water. This was the first day that I hadn't found any place to buy a hot meal. But, I ate prodigious quantities of the Uyghur bread and sausage. Probably, my body was making up for what it had lost in sickness. Doing a pinch test on my middle, I would have to say that I was losing weight. You wouldn't think that a steady diet of bread and goat's meat could trim the fat off of you. Perhaps this would become a new fad back home. *The Uyghur Diet.*

They were able to sell the Atkins diet because it promoted the eating of fatty foods, most notably meat and dairy, which were probably the foods fat people were already eating. I actually heard people say, "This Atkins diet is great. I don't have to modify what I am eating, hardly at all." "Well, then how would you lose weight?" I asked. My Uyghur diet, on the surface, would seem like an easy sale. But in the end, it probably wouldn't work.

I imagined a scene from the Uyghur Weight Loss Clinic in Midtown Manhattan.

Me (as a weight loss consultant): On the Uyghur diet I lost ten kilos, in one week. And you can too, for just $19.95.

Prospective client: That sounds great. I would love to lose that much weight. But do I have to cut back on the things I like?

Me: No, not at all. You get to eat as much bread and goat as you want.

Prospective client: That's good news, because, you know, being a New Yorker, I love my goat. Is there anything else to it?

Me: Well, just a little bit more. For one thing, you have to suffer through some smelly, painful bouts of diarrhea.

Client, not thrilled, but still listening: I guess that would be OK. Anything else?

≡73

Me: And you have to relocate to the Taklamakan Desert.

Client: The Gobi Desert? Do they get a lot of first run Broadway shows there?

Me: I could check for you.

Client: Anything else?

Me: Have you ever done a stationary bicycle at the gym?

Client: Yes, I do twenty minutes a day. But I am still fat.

Me: The good news is, this program will let you lose weight on a bicycle. But the bad news is, you have to pedal fourteen hours a day.

This last bit is where the client would call me a *Momo*, and storm out of my office. People just don't want to put in the time and effort necessary for permanent weight loss.

There was a nice breeze in these tunnels, as the wind was gathered and channeled, running right across my body. I stared up at the ceiling of my cave, with my mind chewing over a million thoughts. The first one was the rather existential question, which both Arthur Rimbaud and Bruce Chatwin had asked themselves, namely, *What the hell am I doing here*? Seriously, this place was both interesting and beautiful, but why was I here? Why was I anywhere – Taiwan, the Shaolin Temple...? What was it all about? And would I write this? Was there a story here at all? Ok, so, Antonio rode his bicycle. Big deal! Lots of people ride bicycles every day, and no one makes a book about it.

Would Tom Cruise play me in the movie? God, I hoped not. I'd be honored if it were Johnny Depp.

My thoughts often digressed a lot in the desert. The desert was like one very huge version of Dr. Timothy Leary's sensory deprivation tank. Devoid of outside stimuli, the consciousness turned inward, creating hallucinatory effects. Some called it just plain going crazy. As much as I didn't know why I was out there, I hoped it was a *beginning,* and not an *end* to adventure. With each new trip, I hoped to raise the bar, not just merely clear the obstacle.

Xinjkiang was once an independent country called East Turkistan

It was hard to believe this was China

The desert was the site of adventure and intrigue since the days of British Empire

I was travelling in the footsteps of Sven Hedin and Marco Polo

Brooklyn had never seemed so far away

The road just went on and on, and I was hot and thirsty

The Chinese people who took this photo were so excited to have met a crazy foreigner. But they didn't believe for a second that I would cross the desert.

I chose a three wheeeled rickshaw because of the luggage compartmnent in the back. I loaded it up with food and water, and I just went.

I made camp inside of the drainage tunnels under the railway

He asked me for a copy of the photo. I would have been happy to send him one but he didn't know his address.

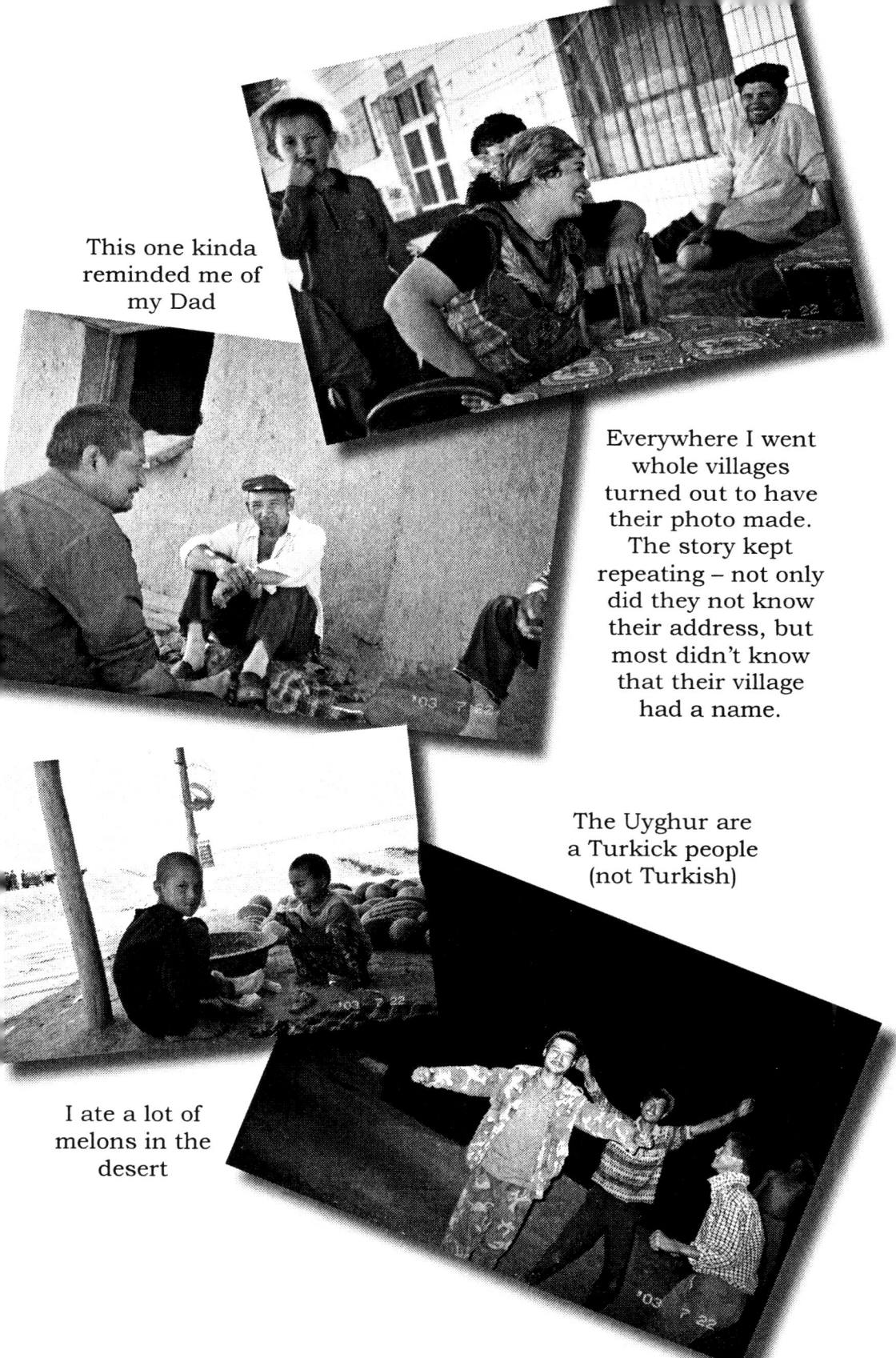

This one kinda reminded me of my Dad

Everywhere I went whole villages turned out to have their photo made. The story kept repeating – not only did they not know their address, but most didn't know that their village had a name.

The Uyghur are a Turkick people (not Turkish)

I ate a lot of melons in the desert

6

The next morning I woke up knowing that I had had a good night's sleep, but still not feeling very fresh. The trip was beginning to wear me down. I wondered, once again, how people survived on lengthy trips of one month or several months. Since I eventually wanted to cycle the whole Chinese coast and possibly row a boat around Taiwan, I worried that I wasn't cutout for trips of such great magnitude.

After only four days, I was beginning to wish it were over. I was having fantasies of what Kashgar would be like. Eventually, I had built it up in my mind as a kind of paradise. Everything good was in Kashgar. All roads led to Kashgar. They had a big swimming pool filled with ice cream, in Kashgar. You could drink all the fluids in the world in Kashgar, soak in a tub, and then get a ten-hour oil massage. There were hotels with clean sheets and swimming pools. You could skinny dip with beautiful girls. The girls would scrub you clean. And then you could spend a civilized evening, discussing world affairs with well-educated Europeans. The Brits would be understated, drunk, and ironic. The French would take the opposing viewpoint, no matter how inane it was to do so. Aaaaah, Kashgar!

A little after noontime, I stopped at the first Uyghur village I had seen in two days. Just as I was rolling into town, my left rear tire went flat. As I walked my bike, I noticed that there was something unusual about this village. It was a little larger than others I had been in. There were about twenty to twenty-five businesses along either side of the highway. It was surprising to see that there were even one or two with colored lights out front. Normally, there would be one or two trucks taking a rest in such a village. But this village seemed to have an inordinate number of truck visitors. This made me a little suspicious. What was different about this town?

A Uyghur woman came running out of a building, wearing only skimpy, pink lingerie. At first I thought she was shouting, as if she needed help. But then I realized that she was giggling hysterically, as if running around outside, nearly naked, was the funniest joke in the world. Up ahead I saw another Uyghur woman in a leopard skin outfit, drinking with some truckers. This was apparently a desert brothel town, which I am sure worked for them. But it was well below the standards of the red light district of any evil town I had ever been in. For one thing, everyone was just as filthy here as they were in the rest of the desert. For another, there were no bars. The leopard skin lady and her trucker friends were sitting on milk crates, drinking *Bai Jo*, white liquor, from the bottle.

There were some businesses that looked like the public showers that I had seen in other parts of China. The prospect of a very long, hot shower, followed by a long massage was appealing. But I knew beyond a doubt, that in a town like this they would offer me a girl, or even just make the assumption that I waned one. And in my present state of loneliness, I would be powerless to refuse. Afterwards, I would probably wake up dead, infected, broke, or all three. I skipped the shower.

Using the Italian order of priorities, I decided to eat first, take a nap, and let the rest sort itself out. I ate a huge meal of goat's meat, mixed with vegetables, served over Uyghur noodles. Excellent! At each of these restaurant stops, I usually drank several pots of tea or several bowls of soup. Afterwards, I lay on the couch and fell asleep. When I woke up, a huge party came in to have lunch, all very curious about the big stranger lying on the couch. I noticed that one of the women in the party was the pink negligee lady I had seen while coming into town. Her bottom was covered now by a skirt. But her top was still the pink negligee. The TV was broadcasting a show in, what I assume, was Uyghur language. I wondered if China offered a Uyghur station, or if it was coming all the way from Turkmenistan.

I am given to understand that the languages of Turkey, Turkmenistan, and several of the former Soviet Republics of Central Asia are quite similar. In particular, the language of Turkmenistan is the closest to Uyghur. But the writing systems of the languages have been changed, for political reasons. Turkey uses a modified Latin script. China allowed the Uyghur to keep their alphabet. For this reason, the Uyghur language of Xinjiang uses the Arabic alphabet. Russia, on the other hand, did not allow its former vassal states to keep their alphabet. For this reason, in Turkmenistan, the Cyrilic alphabet is used. (At the time of this writing, Turkmenbashi, the ruler of Turkmenistan, has been talking of doing away with the Cyrilic script.)

As a linguistic side note, Mongolian is spoken in both Inner and Outer Mongolia. But once again, the Chinese allowed the Inner Mongolians to keep their writing system. The Russians forced Outer Mongolia to adopt the Cyrillic alphabet. In Fall of 2002, Taiwan granted independence to Outer Mongolia. (This is not a misprint. For explanation, buy my book, *Brooklyn Boy in Taiwan.*) But the many years of Russian domination had left most Mongolians unable to read or write Mongolian script. So, the only place in the world where the Mongolian alphabet is still used is Inner Mongolia, which still belongs to China.

The owner of the restaurant, who also doubled as the cook, noticed the flat on my bicycle, and gesticulated madly that I should repair it. Neither he nor his family spoke more than a few words of Chinese. I got reluctantly up from the couch, and showed him the pump and things that I had in the back. He motioned for me to change the tire. But I honestly had no clue how to work on a three-wheeler. He called his son out to help me. On his instructions, I took all my luggage out, and flipped the bike over. The two of them went to work, and within minutes it was good as new. I thanked them, and wasn't sure if I should give them money. Since I hadn't paid my restaurant bill, I figured they would just tack on the repair.

I made a sign that I wanted to pay my check and leave. But the owner pointed up at the sun, as if to say that it was still too high. He motioned to the couch and pillowed his head on his arms, as if sleeping. He didn't have to twist my arm. I went back to the couch, stretched out, and fell into a half sleep. When I woke up the second time the restaurant owner and his family were eating. The son talked to me, as best he could, in broken Chinese. He told me that Kashgar was 240 km away. I hoped I could make it in four more days. But a lot would depend on how many miles I could do after lunch.

There was a documentary, on the Uyghur channel, about the history of the *Tour De France*. Although I knew not a single word of the language, the international words and the names of places and people were discernable. They ran through all of my Tour De France heroes, like Bernard Hinault and Greg LeMond. Greg has since become the forgotten American. He was the first American ever to win the Tour. He won twice. But most people don't know his name today. When they got to Lance Armstrong, the modern champion, from Texas, I nearly wept. I love Lance. He is a major hero and inspiration to me.

When I was injured at the Shaolin Temple, I lay on my bed and read his book, *It's Not About the Bike*, which told the story of his epic battle with cancer. After having won the Tour once, the disease nearly took his life. Doctors had given him a ninety percent probability that he would die, and a zero probability that he would ever ride a bicycle again, much less compete. He has since won the Tour three more times, giving him a total of four wins. If he won again in 2003, which he was planning to do, he would tie the record of five wins. On that day, in Xinjiang, even with the language barrier, I understood that Lance was way ahead. (By the time I got home to Taiwan, I discovered that Lance had indeed won the Tour De France, for the fourth time. CONGRATULATIONS LANCE ARMSTRONG!) If he could pull it off again, in 2004, he would accomplish what no other person had done – six wins in the Tour De France.

When I was a young racer, heroes like Greg LeMond were a big influence on me. Seeing Lance Armstrong while I was on a bicycle trip was extremely motivating. Seeing him here, in China's Xinjiang Province, and in the Uyghur language, was extremely uncanny. Probably it was fate giving me a little push.

Before I left, I asked the restaurant owner to pose in a photo with me. He looked great, about sixty years old, balding, with a huge gray mustache. He posed, but with a bit of hesitancy, which I attributed to his religious beliefs or his general mistrust of foreigners. He shouted at his son in Uyghur. The son ducked into the house and returned with the father's hat and jacket. He put them on and gave me a signal, as if saying, "OK, now you can take pictures."

When I had finished my shots, the son translated

for his father. "He wants to know if you can send us the pictures after you get home?"

"Sure," I said, not expecting to be asked. It was no problem, really. I would jut copy a few prints and drop them in the mail to him. "Could you write down your address for me?" I asked.

The son looked confused. He translated for the father. There was a lot of talk going back and forth. Eventually, what I realized was that he didn't recognize the Chinese word for address.

"I have to write on the envelope the place I am sending the photos," I explained.

"You can send here," said the son, simply.

"I understand that. But I don't know where here is. Could you write the place for me?"

The son wrote one word, in Uyghur script, and handed me the paper.

"No, I mean like, could you write your name, the village name, the street name, and the numbers?"

Now the lights went on. The son ran in the house, probably to confer with the rest of his family. It occurred to me that they probably didn't send letters very often, if at all. With all of their relatives here in this one village, there would be no need. He returned later, with what I assumed was the proper address, written out very neatly, in Uyghur script.

"Excellent!" I said. "Now, could you write it again in Chinese?" Mail in China was so dodgy anyway. There was no way that I believed a letter, with an address written in Uyghur, mailed from Hong Kong, would ever arrive here in the desert.

The son just shrugged his shoulders. His reaction wasn't just that he couldn't write Chinese, but that he didn't have the concept that this place, and all of the people in it, could also be written in Chinese. He was Uyghur. The place was Uyghur. How would you write that in Chinese?

I knew I was lying when I assured him that I would mail the letter.

I left the restaurant at 3:30 and rode until after 8:30. This was the longest I had ridden. I saw a jackrabbit that day, which along with a single black vulture, were the only non-domesticated animals I saw during the entire trip. The vulture may even have come because of me. I knew there were times when I looked like I was close to death.

My knee was beginning to act up quite severely, and I was jut getting tired of the journey in general. Kashgar was sounding awfully good to me. If at lunchtime I only had two hundred forty kilometers to go, by the time I stopped for the night I only had two hundred kilometers left. I could do that in two very hard days, if I pushed. Of course, there was still the fact that I didn't know for sure if the two hundred forty figure was accurate. In my pack I carried a stack of papers and research a Hong Kong friend, Joseph, had downloaded off of the Internet for me. Among other things, it contained about five maps of the region. Not one of them had enough reliable information to be of any use.

Joseph had said to me, "If you don't know where you are going, maybe you should postpone the trip till you have better information."

My answer was that I honestly believed that I had all of the information that was available. Good information just didn't exist. If I waited, I would be no smarter, just older.

No matter what the actual distance was, I had half – or close to half – of the journey behind me. By eliminating my long nap at lunchtime, and riding until 9:00 PM, I would be able to do about fifty percent more miles in a day. Another way of saying it was that every two days on my new schedule would represent one less night that I would have to sleep in a cave.

I lay in my cave, on my side, too knackered even to fish my food and water out of my pack. I had gotten a little crazy in the sun that day, singing songs non-stop. What I usually did on these kinds of trips was pick a theme, say songs about the sea, and sing as many as I could think of. Today, alcohol songs kept me busy for several hours. I sang *Margarita Ville, Tequila Sunrise, One Whisky, One Burbon and One Beer* – the George Thoroughgood version – and *Escape,* also called *The Pina Colada Song.* Just to be fair to my country roots, I also sang *Give Me Two Pina Coladas* by Garth Brooks.

Next I did 70's sitcom themes – *Alice, Welcome Back Cater, Mary Tyler More, The Courtship of Eddy's Father, F-Troop, Giligan's Island, WKRP in Cincinnati,* and *All in the Family.* I did that one twice, because I like to do the different voices. Of course that led to *The Jeffersons.* Also on the repertoire were *Silvers Spoons* and that show with Michael J. Fox.

I was reminded of the movie *Ishtar,* where Dustin Hoffman and Warren Beatty, an aspiring pop duo, were playing a gig in Morocco. The movie wasn't very good. But, it had a few funny moments. The two were lost, out in the desert, with no water, nearing death, the vultures were circling, and suddenly, Dustin Hoffman says, "I got an idea for a song." Warren Beatty joins in, and down on their knees, only moments left to live, they start singing in terrible harmony.

I also liked the movie *The Three Amigos,* where Steve Martin, Chevy Chase, and Martin Short are lost in the desert. Steve and Chevy are dying of thirst. Martin Short takes his own canteen and drinks generously. Then he gargles with gallons of water and spits it out in front of the dying men. Steve Martin and Chevy Chase are staring at him, hoping that he will offer them some water. But when Martin Short finishes gargling, he throws the half full canteen away and begins applying Chap Stick to his lips. As the water runs into the sand, he turns to his friends and says, "Would you like some lip balm?"

Yeah, dying of thirst is pretty funny in the movies.

Remembering the brothel town I had been earlier in the day, a flicker of regret passed through my mind. I had left because it was too perilous. But maybe I could have stood just a little bit of peril.

Whether it took me three days or only two to reach Kashgar, I knew that I would be among people again soon, so I was more concerned about my appearance than I had been. In the morning I shaved off my heavy beard, which required five bottles of my drinking water. I also rode shirtless for two hours to even out my tan line.

As I am a huge fan of show tunes, I often kill time on my trips by singing the entire score of a musical, such as *Les Misérable* or *Rent*. Les Mis seemed extremely appropriate to the desert. It starts with the convicts laboring and singing.

Look down, look down, don't look them in the eye. Look down. Look down. You're here until you die. The sun is high. It's hot as hell below. Look down. Look down. There's twenty years to go.

I always changed the "twenty years to go" part to "two hundred and forty kilometers to go." Or more accurately, "some unknown quantity of kilometers to go."

Near the end of the first act is the protest song.

Can you hear the people sing? Singing the songs of angry men. It is the music of a people who would not be slaves again.

This song always made me choke up a little. But

≡89

now it had very special meaning for me, as it was the theme song of the historic protest in Hong Kong, on July first, when the people of Hong Kong stood up to a lessening of their first amendment rights by the Beijing government. Every time I hear that song now, I am back in Victoria Park, one small voice, in a sea of people, on the hottest day of the year.

Why did I go to the desert? Why did I go to Shaolin? Why do I live with no fixed address? Why don't I write about nice hotels and breathtaking scenery like other travel writers?

The answer is that the reasons for living, the very drive to take another, breath come from the human drama played out between people. The fear, the tension, the hatred, and the hope that encompassed Hong Kong on that day, that permeated every aspect of the human condition, branded me with an indelible mark. And I will carry that memory, so vivid as to experience brief instances of time travel, for the rest of my life.

The desert was the same way. I knew that things would happen there. I would experience emotions and sensations, tastes and smells, that would forever transport me back to Xinjiang. And the special thing about this type of neurological programming is that it remains with you indefinitely. When I am a hundred and seventy-five years old, a forgotten soul, sitting alone in the corner of some state run retirement facility, the smell of goat meat, or the feeling of the hot dry sun on my head, or the feeling of saddle sores, or the smell of sun block, or the gritty feeling of fine powdery dust in my parched throat, or maybe a clear, starless night, will remind me of when I was young and strong, and I rode across the Taklamakan Desert.

Maybe I had had too much sun that day. But those were the thoughts that carried me off to sleep.

Shortly after sunrise I stopped to make a photo of

a Uyghur man sitting atop a huge pile of hay, on the back of a hose drawn cart. I thought the man was staring at me strangely because of my appearance or because of the camera. But then I heard a loud *CRASH!* behind me. The man had been staring, because while I was taking his photo, my bike had been rolling, very slowly, to the edge of the road. I turned just in time to see my bike smack the embankment, bounce, fall, smack the embankment again, flip over, and come to rest, upside down, fifteen feet below. The cart rode past me, and I missed my shot.

By this point I was so exhausted and so fed up with the trip, that if the bike had been broken, I would simply have left it there and hitched a ride to Kashgar. Making it most of the way to Kashgar would still have been a good story. I collected my gear, which had been thrown all over the desert, and piled it on the shoulder of the road. I righted the bike, and began pushing it back up the embankment. One problem with the rickshaw was that it was much heavier than a bicycle. In fact, I could not quite lift the entire rickshaw off of the ground. Attempts to man-handle it usually resulted in one or the other of the wheels still making contact with the ground and thwarting any efforts to manipulated the bike into a better position.

The grade was just too steep, and the surface too soft. I got it almost all of the way to the top, but couldn't quite clear the last few feet. Straining like the Grinch who stole Christmas, I pushed and pushed that sled, but it just kept rolling back, threatening to break loose and go crashing down the hill a second time. Suddenly, out of nowhere, a Uyghur man appeared, carrying a shovel and a hoe over his shoulder. He dropped his farm implements, grabbed the handlebars, and pulled me over the hump. Without his help I honestly would not have been able to rescue the bike.

I thanked him a million times, but he just smiled and smiled, happy to have been able to help. I think, too, he was pretty excited to meet a foreigner. He took up his tools and disappeared into the desert, on whatever business he had. I knew nothing of agriculture, but I could not imagine that one could make a great living by farming in the desert. These were resilient people.

The bike appeared to be OK. But when I turned the pedals, the wheels did not move. What could I do? I sat down on my pack, drank some water, ate some sausage, and weighed out my options. One option was to push the bike to the next town. But the deeper I got into the desert, the further apart the towns were. Straining my eyes, I could see nothing, other than sand, between myself and the horizon. OK, plan B. I could quit, and hitch a ride on a truck. Straining my eyes in the other direction, I saw nothing but sand between myself and the other horizon. It could be hours before a big truck came through there.

While I was pondering what to do, a Uyghur family passed me in one of their strange, motorcycle drawn carts. I saw the break lights come on, and they backed up. A young man got out and in broken Chinese said, "I know you."

"You know me?" I asked, surprised.

"Yes," he said. "You bought 20 bottles of water and a Coke from my father two days ago. Then you took pictures of me and my family."

That certainly sounded like something I would do. At the time I didn't recognize him. When I got back to Hong Kong and compared the photos, sure enough, he was right. It was the same guy. What were the odds of that?

He asked to take a look at my bike. Flipping it over, I was amazed at how simple the mechanism was. The two rear wheels were on a fixed axle, with a single, very small gear, in the center, where the chain attached. The axle rested on a rail, with several inches of play in either direction. The young man loosened the nuts, held the axle in place, and then shifted it rearwards, until the chain was taut. He tightened the nuts, and that was it. I was good to go.

"How many kilometers you go?" he asked.

"Three hundred," I said, proudly.

His voice took an admonishing tone. "You must tighten the chain every fifty kilometers. Even small children know that."

"Sorry," I said, sheepishly.

"Maybe it is better I drive you," he said.

"No thanks."

He seemed genuinely worried about leaving me alone in the desert, especially since I knew so little about my bike.

"You could ride with my family," he offered.

Although the young man and his father had come out to help me, the women remained inside of the vehicle, with the curtains drawn. Periodically, I saw a curious eye peering out at me.

He offered several more times to drive me. But I refused. Reluctantly, he left. I had just gotten underway again, when I saw a cyclist coming towards me. I was so surprised to see a bicycle out here, that I almost let him slip by without even a wave. In fact, my brain was so conditioned to only seeing Uyghur, and the occasional Chinese, that I nearly didn't register the fact that he was a Westerner.

"STOP!" I cried out, as I came to my senses.

The baffled cyclist turned around, coming to halt beside me.

"Sorry," I said. "I wasn't sure if you were a Westerner." This may have seemed a little strange, since he was over six feet tall, blond, and had blue eyes.

"I thought you might be a Westerner because of the Yankee cap," he said, in a German accent. "But because of your bike I thought you might be Uyghur."

We chatted for a while, swapping stories. Martin, as he was called, had apparently been on the road for thirteen months. He had left his home in Switzerland and ridden east, crossing all of Europe and riding into India. He rode across India and then attempted to enter China through Tibet, but was denied entry. So, he had to return to India, cut north, and enter China through Pakistan. That one bit of bad luck had cost him nearly two months.

Martin was a real adventurer. He had covered the entire Karakorum Highway, something I also wanted to do. I told him that my real dream was to cross from Hotan to Aksu with camels.

"How long does that take?" he asked.

"About forty five days," I answered.

"Humm," he said, as if thinking it over. I honestly believe that had we been closer to either Hotan or Aksu, I could have convinced him to come with me.

"How far are you planning to go?" I asked.

"That depends on football," he said, with a laugh.

"What?"

"Well, I will continue on to Aksu, then cut southeast, toward Vietnam. I should be arriving at the Vietnam border around the time of the World Cup. If my team makes it to the playoffs I will go home to watch it. If not, I will just keep going."

"Man! You Europeans really like football," I joked.

Martin smiled. "It's not really that I love football so much. It's just that you have to stop at some point. I quit my job more than a year ago. I was making a lot of money, but I was very unhappy. I had never ridden a bicycle further than to the grocery store and back.

94■

But I got on and headed east. When I started, I had no idea how far I was going. I just rode. It felt good. It still feels good. So, I continue riding. If I don't set some kind of deadline, like the World Cup, then I will just ride forever."

I was impressed, and also humbled.

"How far are you going?" he asked.

"To Kashgar, I said, meekly.

"I know that. I meant after Kashgar."

"Home."

"Oh."

We exchanged email addresses, and parted ways.

A while later, a truck stopped, and two Chinese truck drivers invited me to share their lunch with them. We sat at the side of the road, on small cushions, in the shade of the truck, and ate melon and bread. Melon is eaten all the time here to curb thirst and stave off hunger.

The younger trucker told me that he was twenty-eight years old. He had a wife and two children, and they lived with the wife's family in an apartment in Aksu.

"I make, every day two round trips to Kashgar." he told me. "Normal truckers do one, and then they sleep, or drink, or go with the girls. With one trip, can support the family. But I do two, and save money. In three years, I will buy my own truck, and get to keep all the money."

I felt proud of him. He knew what he wanted, and he was making it happen.

"My children speak good Chinese. They also learn the English in school. They will go to university," he said, proudly.

This was the new economy. If there were nothing else you could say about a capitalist system, it allowed people to dream. Somehow, in a communist system, where everyone was the same, everyone was dirt poor and had nothing to look forward to. At least in a market economy it was possible to pull yourself up. And, it wasn't like this guy had been handed an opportunity that was unavailable to others. He said himself, *The other truckers make one trip, and then sleep.*

The truckers offered me a lift. Everyone offered me a lift. They just didn't get it.

"It is only one hundred twenty kilometers to Kashgar," he said. "You could put your bike in the back and be in Atuchi tonight. You could have a shower and a good night's sleep. Then you could ride to Kashgar in the morning."

It sounded tempting, but I stuck to my guns and politely refused.

Twenty minutes later, I regretted not accepting their offer of a ride, because I left them and rode right into hell. It was my first sandstorm. It wasn't quite an official sandstorm, but there was a twenty-mile an-hour head wind, which pelted me with sand, and lasted for five hours. The wind was so strong, I had to walk most of the way dragging my bike. Unfortunately, the big bike acted as a sail. When my grip weakened, the bike actually blew away from me.

To make matters worse, parts of the highway were under construction. I had the misfortune of running into the sandstorm at one of the points where there was a detour onto a gravel road. Now I had gravel added to the mix of pebbles and desert dust that were sandblasting my face. I could hear the sharp projectiles colliding with my sunglasses, like sleet on a windshield. I didn't want to imagine what would have happened if I hadn't been wearing eye protection. The gravel rolled underfoot, causing me to stumble, and causing the wheels of my bike to foul.

The air was so thick and hot, at times it felt like

walking into a hair dryer, or the exhaust end of a jet engine. At other times it was like walking into a force field. I could lean almost all of the way over, but the air supported me.

The combined exertion of fighting the wind and negotiating the gravel left me gasping for air, forcing the fine dust down in my lungs. Panting caused my tongue and the inside of my mouth to become covered in dust. My mouth dried out in the arid wind. My tongue felt like a garden slug covered in salt. It began to wither and die. As I hadn't seen a village all day, I hadn't had a chance to refill my water supply. Only five 600 ml bottles remained, just enough for a few hours. I cursed myself for wasting so much water shaving the previous day.

It was so hot sandy and awful. At the very moment that I needed to drink more than usual, I had to abstain from drinking at all. It was the closest to hell that I came.

An old man appeared, selling melons from the back of a horse drawn cart. I bought one for 4 RMB, and tore into it with my pocketknife, eating greedily. The melon helped a lot, but I needed to drink. I also needed the security of having a number of bottles on hand.

I didn't experience real thirst on this trip. I mean, I don't know what it is to be lost in the desert for two days with no water, or set adrift in a lifeboat. But I got a glimpse of thirst, and I must say it was infinitely worse than hunger. Where hunger can make you lightheaded, weak, and dizzy, thirst is an active pain, which eats at you. Where hunger would make you lay down, go to sleep, and die, thirst would make you writhe in agony. It could drive you insane. I imagined that thirst made one feel the way a heroin addict felt. You wouldn't break into a house out of hunger, but you would sell out your best friend because of thirst.

I passed through a village, too small to have a store or restaurant. A little boy rode beside me on his bicycle, and I asked him where I could get water. He disappeared, returning with a bucket full of water. I wasn't sure how clean it was, so I was afraid to drink it. On the other hand, this was a dire emergency. My compromise was to drink one of the bottles from my supply, and then refill the empty with the water the boy gave me. I would drink this potentially fetid water when all my clean water was gone.

Outside of town there was a Chinese work gang, who I asked for water. Incredibly, they had none. This was so typical of the Chinese. I didn't know how they did it. They could work indefinitely with neither food nor water. At the Shaolin Temple, for an eight-hour training day, we were only allowed one liter of water per person, and this was both for drinking and for washing. And I was the only one who ever complained.

There was a well-dressed Chinese man sitting in a pickup truck, who must have been some type of bureaucrat, sent to check on the progress of the workers. He gave me all the water he had – one, partially drunk, 600 ml bottle. I drained it down my throat, then bought another melon from a vendor.

Gradually, the storm abated. All at once, the wind disappeared. The sky remained dusty for the next two days, but the danger was over. I desperately needed food and water, but was still in the middle of nowhere. Although I didn't see any restaurants, I stopped in the first village I came to. It was merely a collection of three or four houses made of earth. A fat man sat on a rug, talking with the other men, as I approached. I asked for food, and the man gave me a melon, which

I ate greedily. His two young sons squatted beside us, eating all of the melons, which were overripe.

An Uyghur family pulled up in a motorcycle driven rickshaw. To my surprise, the driver was the guy who had stopped to help me when my bike broke down. Coincidence was rife in the desert.

The boys were covered in months and months of caked-on dust and sand, but they were cute. They dug into the melons with the same excitement that Western kids would have. The older boy, who was about ten, was wielding a knife as big as his head, feeding pieces to the younger boy, who was probably about four. What amazes me in these one staple cultures is that they never grow tired of the local food. How can this be? I liked melon quite a lot. But if it was the only thing I had to eat, day in and day out, I would be pretty sick of it. These boys were enjoying that melon so much you would think it was the first one they had eaten in a year, rather than the first one they had eaten since breakfast.

At Shaolin Temple, I remember having lengthy discussions with my friends about how delicious rice was. They ate rice three times a day, their whole lives, and yet they loved it.

The father and I talked for a few minutes, but hunger and thirst were still gnawing at me. So I needed to go. When I asked him how much? His answer was *Shi quai chien.* The first word sounded like four, which would have been normal for a melon. But with his accent, it could also have been ten. I asked him to repeat, and sure enough, he was asking for ten. This was highway robbery. On some other day, I would have fought. But on that day, I was just too tired. His son's eyes grew as I handed him the ten quai note. I knew it was wrong. The father knew it was wrong. The son gasped, definitely knowing it was wrong. What annoyed me most was the smug look on the father's face. He was so proud of himself for overcharging me. To this day, I curse myself for not having protested or outright refused. But as I said, I was too tired. In my uncharitable heart, I remember thinking, *He over charged me by about fifty cents.* Another way of saying it was that his integrity was worth fifty cents. Or still another way of saying it was, for less than the money that I could find under the cushions in the couch, I could coerce him to theft. I controlled him.

Of course, I had been in the sun a long time, and wasn't thinking straight. When I turned to go, the father acted like I was a guest, leaving too soon.

"You're going?" he asked, sounding almost hurt.

"Of course," I said. I wanted to add, *Because you stole my money.* But I didn't.

I came to another Uyghur village where I bought eighteen bottles of water, for my supply, and drank five more.

Later, in a larger village, I stopped for a hot meal and a rest. At first, the villagers were standoffish, as if they were afraid of me. But little by little, they began to gather around the restaurant and ask me questions. Timidly I took out my camera, half expecting the mood to change, to one that was less welcoming. Instead, the villagers all spoke at once, saying, "Take my picture." Soon, the entire village lined up. And I photographed every man, woman, and child in the village. At least one woman came with her small baby and asked me to make a photo of her.

For some strange reason, there was one very drunk, very rowdy Russian living in the village with his Uyghur wife.

"He is from the same place you are," said the wife.

"You mean Brooklyn?" I asked, knowing full well that I hadn't told them where I was from.

"Yes...no...you know. That place you come from," she explained.

I honestly don't know for certain that the guy was Russian. I tried talking to him, but he couldn't speak Chinese. He looked Russian. And former Soviet citizens – and maybe a few Cubans, Angolans, or Mozambiquans – would have been the only non-Asians permitted to immigrate to China. Since he wasn't black or Hispanic, I was guessing Russian. But to these simple Uyghur, there was only *here*, and everything else was *over there*. Since he was not from here, he had to be from over there. And, as I must also be from over there, we must know each other and speak the same language. I guess, from their point of view, it made sense.

When I had finished, the people asked if I would send them the photos. Once again, I asked for the address. The man who was the spokesperson for the town said, "Don't you know the address?"

"No."

"Then how did you come here?"

I didn't have an answer for this one. I asked two more times. Finally the man wrote something on the paper.

"This is my name. Just give all the pictures to me, and I will see that they get to the right people."

For the second time in the desert, I told a lie.

"OK. I'll send them as soon as I get back to Hong Kong."

Around 9:30 PM, I wandered by a Uyghur work camp, and the foreman waved me over. The camp was on the new highway being constructed, several hundred meters away from the old road I was walking on. I left my bike on the old road and walked over to the foreman. He asked me where I had come from and where I was going. Then he invited me to stay the night, which I gratefully accepted. Where the Chinese workers slept inside of tents, the Uyghur slept outdoors. They spread two filthy, smelly blankets out on a gravel pile for me and told me to take a rest, while they sent their youngest worker to fetch my bike. The blankets reeked. I reeked. The Uyghur reeked. But it didn't matter. Once again, I was reminded of how bad we all smelled at The Shaolin Temple. It was just part of life in rural China.

I had misgivings about someone else trying to ride my bike, because it was so hard to control. But, I figured that they were Uyghur and knew how to handle a bike. Also, I was so tired I almost didn't care. I lay down on the most comfortable bed I had had since coming to the desert and instantly fell asleep. Suddenly, the whole camp erupted in laughter. I opened one eye, and saw that the young Uyghur had just driven my bike off of an eight-foot embankment. Several grinning men ran out to help him back onto the road. A few minutes later, he drove my bike off of a twelve-foot embankment. He now held the record for the highest embankment fall. And the outdoor record for the most falls in one day.

When the battered boy brought my bike into camp, the men immediately stripped it down, completely, adjusted the tension, adjusted the gears and brakes, and oiled the chain. When they were finished, it was better than new. These Uyghur were amazing.

Dinner was an excellent bowl of Uyghur noodles with meat and vegetables. After dark, one of the Uyghur produced a traditional stringed instrument, similar to a large balalaika, called a *duodar*. He sang a slow, soul full tune which most likely reminded the men of home. Another Uyghur accompanied him, playing drums on an empty paint tub. Soon, all the men were doing a dance, which looked like the way my

Turkish friends danced back in Germany.

Construction workers dancing together? It looked suspiciously like *The Village People* live in concert. They had bought me dinner. I was hoping they didn't expect me to put out.

The leader extended his hand to me, and I joined him. We spun, and kicked, and jumped. We danced and whirled out in the desert, under a huge sky, where the stars burned as bright as reading lights. It was magic, and definitely the happiest moment of the trip.

When the dance had finished, we all lay down on our gravel piles and slept. A cool breeze soothed us, while the heavens directed a laser-light show overhead. 9-11 was forgotten. My Muslim friends lay all about me, accepting, protecting, sharing. It was the best night's sleep that I had the entire trip, maybe ever.

7

The Uyghur gave me breakfast, but also gave me some bad news. I was still one hundred forty-five kilometers away from Kashgar. As much as I wanted not to believe them, I suspected that they were right. After I left the Uyghur camp, I decided I was finished with sleeping on the ground. My goal was to push through, one hundred kilometers to Atuchi, and sleep in a hotel.

The day grew hotter, and the strain of more than a week of arduous travel was wearing me down like a leaden suit. By evening, I could not think straight any longer. My mind only retained one thought – *Must get to Atuchi. Must get to Atuchi.*

A father and son called me over to their wagon full of melons and gave me one. It was another of the moments that would keep me going when I thought I could go no more.

My body was so depleted that I drank constantly. I just always had an open bottle in my hand while riding. When I finished, I tossed it away and took a fresh one. The sun seemed more intense now, although the desert began to give way. As I approached Atuchi, and later Kashgar, there was a bit of sporadic vegetation, almost looking like a step rather than a proper desert.

I rode right through lunch, stopping for less than fifteen minutes to swallow some food. Around 5:00 PM, I made another stop by a father and his young son sitting under an umbrella selling drinks. The father was extremely fat, as were some of the men in the desert. This probably came from their survival instinct, which taught them to sit still as much as possible. He only moved to take my money and hand me my drinks. Even then, he had an incredible economy of motion. What must he have thought of someone insane enough to ride a bicycle in the desert heat? Maybe he had never ridden a bicycle even once in his life. He had probably never been jogging, and probably never played football.

I drank three bottles of juice and continued on. The next twenty kilometers were hellish. I really felt I could take no more. The thought of just stopping and sleeping right where I was crossed my mind several times. But I pushed myself to continue. Eventually, I crested a hill and saw a sign, which read *Kashgar 42 km.* The sign also said that there was another town, three kilometers off the main road, at the next left hand turn. Unfortunately, I had never seen Atuchi written, so I couldn't recognize the Chinese characters. If this town was or was not Atuchi, was not at all relevant. I just needed a town.

The dearth of signs in China was appalling. But even when signs were present, they were often impossible to follow. First of all, because of their writing system, the Chinese think in pictures, not words. Also, the Chinese characters were traditionally written in columns, from top to bottom and from right to left. This makes it very difficult for Westerners to understand, for example, when Chinese give us a series of instruction. The Westerner would not be clear as to which operation was to be done first. In speaking Chinese, the steps might be given in an order that seemed inverted to us. By the same token, the street signs often asked us to make turns where there were none, or to turn in some way that seemed contrary to logic.

One more problem with getting around in China was that street signs in communist countries just suck, plain and simple. Every dollar wasted on street signs is one less dollar that the minister of manufacturing street signs could use to build his weekend house. And of course, there is the paranoia factor. If there were good street signs, then when another army invaded, they would be able to find Atuchi.

An invading army may have been able to find Atuchi, but I could not. The sign said turn left. At the place where it wanted me to turn left there was only a huge rice patty. It was three more kilometers to what appeared to be a major highway junction. But it was completely devoid of signage. To make matters worse, the highway had two service roads running beside it. So, even if I guessed that this was the place to turn, I didn't know if I needed the highway or the service road. This was all just too much thinking for my brain, which was thick with fatigue and too much sun.

Some young Uyghur men were bathing in an irrigation ditch beside the road. I parked the bike, ran down the embankment, and almost dove in. But the water was completely black and had the consistency of unrefined crude oil. Standing this close to them, I could see the stains the water left on their bodies. Said another way, that water was so dirty that if I was lost in the desert for a week, I wouldn't want to go near it. I had to find Atuchi. I was going to ask the bathing guys, but they didn't look very bright. In fact, they looked very in-bred. I made my way back up the embankment.

A bright-eyed young girl of about thirteen waved me down. I asked her where Atuchi was, but she either wouldn't or couldn't speak Chinese. She ran into the house and returned with her mother, who looked like an evil witch from a fairy tale. Her eyes, which were sunken and black, stared out from a face which was gaunt and sharp like a bird of prey. She was clad all in black, with a black veil draping down from her small, cylindrical hat. Even if her house had been made of gingerbread, I would not have gone with her. But the house was not made of gingerbread. It was a dilapidated shack, ten feet from the road. The door was open, and I could see that they owned almost nothing.

"Which way to Atuchi?" I asked.

She stared at me and then began babbling in Uyghur. Even though I didn't understand a word of what she was saying, I could tell that it was the incoherent ranting of someone who had gone mad. She shouted. She gesticulated. I was just about to pull away, when she started rummaging through the things in the back of my bike. She came up with one of my full, store bought, unopened bottles of water, showed it to me, and then slipped it into her dress. As poor as she was, I was running low on water again, and couldn't part with a full bottle. Then, remembering something, I fished through my things till I found the bottle of tap water the little boy had given me the previous day. I figured this water had to be cleaner than the black sludge I had seen in the town. The woman traded with me gladly.

I rode away, just far enough so I wouldn't have to deal with the crazy woman any longer. She walked out to the center of the road, and stared at me, making my skin crawl. I would have given up at this point, but didn't know how. There was no one to surrender to. Just then, by some bizarre stroke of luck, a young Chinese couple came down the road, in a compact car. I flagged them down, and saw that they were well dressed, clean, and educated, probably the children of some politicos or high-ranking military officers. They pointed me toward Atuchi, and moments later I was cycling down the main street.

As towns went, Atuchi really wasn't bad. The outskirts of town was not a slum or a settlement, as is often the way in the developing world. Instead, it was a suburb, like Long Island, or Northern Virginia. The houses were well-maintained, freestanding dwellings, with a little bit of yard out front. The streets were lined with trees, which gave the place an odd Mayberry feeling. The city proper was also relatively nice, with lots of shops and business. All of the public buildings were well maintained. But because this was still China, the nicest, and by far the largest, buildings were the police and military barracks.

Because I can't read many characters, I have trouble finding the kind of business I am looking for. In other words, without going inside, I don't know if I am looking at a hardware store, a shoe store, or a grocery store. Finding hotels is extremely problematic, because they could also be big fancy KTVs (karaoke lounges), brothels, bathhouses, or some type of resort facility for visiting party members. I stopped at the army base and asked the century on guard duty. Actually, it turned out that it was a fire station. His helmet and the submachine gun with bayonet threw me.

Following the sentry's directions, I came to what I suspected was a hotel. I still wasn't certain, however, because you had to enter through the dinning room. Maybe it was just a restaurant, I thought.

"Do you have any rooms?" I asked the first person I saw, who could have been the waiter or the eye surgeon.

He took one look at me, and suddenly I remembered what I must have looked like. I hadn't bathed in over a week. My skin bore the remains of layer upon layer of sunscreen, caked with salty sweat, mixed with dead bugs, and all neatly rolled in a granular veneer of desert sand. I probably smelled to heaven. And my clothes, which had probably looked new once, a very long time ago, had only been changed once all week. On top of this, I had left my cycle chained up outside, entering the building with my rucksack. This may have given the appearance that I had just walked across the desert. In the old *Kung Fu* TV show, almost every episode began with Quai Chang Kain, David Karradine's character, entering a saloon, all dusty and exhausted, after crossing the desert on foot.

Those spaghetti westerns always had Clint Eastwood walking in out of the desert half dead. He would wander into some dusty little town, and the first thing he did was down a full glass of whisky. Then he would get in a fight and kill half the town. The fact is, you couldn't drink whisky if you were dying of thirst. The smell alone would make you sick. Pouring down your throat, alcohol, a dehydrant, would feel like you were swallowing razor blades. If by some weird twist of fate you manage to swallow the alcohol, your kidneys would probably shut down instantly.

Kwai Chang Kane was no better. He was half dead when he got to town. Then he drank a single glass of water, but it revived him, because he put special, magic, Chinese herbs in it. I wondered if these were the same herbs my Sifu had given me, at the Shaolin Temple, to cure SARS.

"No more rooms," said the clerk.

Feeling like Joseph and Mary, I turned to go, when a woman, who I later found out was the owner's wife, came running over to me.

"How many nights?"

"Just one."

"How many people?"

"Just one."

"Eighty RMB," she said. "In advance."

"No problem. But one thing, I absolutely need to take a shower, several in fact. Does the room have a shower?"

"Yes, of course," she answered. I knew she was lying. I thought through the typical Chinese tricks.

"Does the shower have water?" I asked.

She made a face like *Rats! He figured it out.*

"We can put you in a room with a shower, with water," she said.

"Hot water?"

Now she looked like I was asking for the sun, the moon, and the stars.

"Yes, we can give you a room with hot water."

"Really?" I asked. "Please tell me now. I plan to take about twenty showers. If this is a problem, I can go somewhere else."

Tough words, for a guy who didn't know if there was somewhere else to go.

"Yes, this won't be a problem."

I knew she was lying, but I was too tired to fight.

The woman led me up the stairs, to my room, on the third floor. I made her verify that there was, in fact, a shower. The first problem arose when I asked for my room key.

"It's right here," she said, showing me a humongous ring, which contained the keys to every room in the hotel.

"You mean you want me to put that in my pocket?" I asked.

"No!" she said, as if I were the one who was confused. "You can't have this."

"So, how will I get in and out of my room?"

"The girl will let you in."

"How will I find the girl?"

"You will find her," said the woman, and she walked off.

As much as I didn't relish the idea of wandering up and down the corridors, mumbling *I am the key master of Gozar; give me the key*, it was too late to back out. I had already committed.

The shower, of course, wasn't hot. But by the time I found out, I was standing naked, soaking wet, with shampoo in my eyes. To complain, I would have had to put my clothes back on, go down stairs, find the landlady, listen to her lie, then wait for her to do something about it. In the end I probably would have got tired of waiting and wound up showering cold anyway. Or, I might have gone down the stairs, not found the landlady, and then have to search for the girl with the key. For either scenario I would have needed to dress first. Putting on clothes would have been an issue. My dirty clothes smelled so bad that I didn't want to touch them. Neither did I want to foul my clean clothes by having them come in contact with my unwashed body. So I cut out all of the intervening steps, and took a cold shower.

The amount of sand that came off of my body was staggering. You could have filled every pothole from Union Square to The Empire State Building with the quantity of earth that I left on the bathroom floor. I say on the floor. In China, even in expensive hotels, there is almost never a shower stall or tub. You stand next to the toilet and shower, with all of the water going on the floor. In Taiwan there is usually a drain in the floor. In China there never seemed to be one, so the bathroom always had about three inches of fetid water sitting in it. With the addition of salt and sand from my body, combined with the desert heat, I had just created a swamp environment. It was the world's largest petri dish, a breeding ground for malarial mosquitoes. They will probably have an outbreak of Dengue Fever in Atuchi, and it is my fault. But I didn't care. The biological terror I unleashed on them was my revenge for taking a cold shower.

As much as it felt good to wash, the cold water just couldn't penetrate the oily sunscreen which coated my flesh. The other issue was that in Asia, I have never had a shower where I was standing under a shower-head and able to wash and scrub with both hands. Inevitably, there is a hand held shower wand, and you wind up spraying water with one hand, while washing with the other.

When the shower suddenly stopped working, I could still smell myself. But my thirst and hunger were now reaching emergency status. I needed to eat dinner and drink some fluids before filing a complaint.

The restaurant in the hotel was great. The owners were Chinese, but the head chef – and manager – was Uyghur. He was extremely knowledgeable about the region. His Chinese was excellent, and we had the best conversation I had had since coming to Xinjiang. Once he heard about my trip, he was so excited that he dragged all of the other guests and employees outside to get a look at my bike. They all laughed and commented on how hard the journey must have been.

"Where will you finish?" asked one man.

"In Kashgar, tomorrow."

Suddenly, it was as if they hadn't heard the first part of the story, namely that I had already come five hundred kilometers across the desert, alone.

"But can you make it all the way to Kashgar?" asked one man, genuinely concerned for my safety. "It's over forty kilometers."

"Surely you won't do it alone?" asked someone else.

"What if you got lost?" asked another.

I love the Chinese because they are friendly, and generally easy to talk to. But, they seemed to miss the obvious quite frequently. In their experience, people didn't cross the desert by cycle. And people never went anywhere alone. So, if at the beginning of the journey they told me I couldn't do it, then I would understand.

But now they had information which contradicted their original opinion. Now they knew I had come five hundred kilometers. So, why couldn't they accept that I could go forty kilometers more? It was because their brains just rejected anything that didn't match their preconceived notions.

All countries, all nationalities – in fact, all people, myself included – have this problem to some extent. But the Chinese are completely mired in it. They cannot or will not amend a previously accepted hypothesis, even if new facts are completely contradictory to their assumptions.

I didn't want to argue. My head was woozy, and I was about to collapse at any moment. I thanked them and barely made it back to my seat before everything went black. Through a kind of high pitched whining in my ears, I heard the chef ask me what I wanted to eat.

"Anything Uyghur," I said. "And lots of soup and tea."

At that moment, the chef was my best friend, and the only person on the planet who understood me. By a lot of tea, I meant several pots of tea. And this is what he gave me. He laid three full pots on my table and refilled them as I drank. I think I drank about six of them. I also drank countless bowls of soup. Again, he had the waitress bring me several bowls at a time. Finally, the main course came, but I was only able to eat a little of it, and very slowly. I was unable to stomach a great deal of food.

My experience on these kinds of trips has been that I can only eat so much food at a sitting, so I knew that I would need another meal in an hour or so.

While I picked at my dinner, the cook sat with me and talked. He didn't hate the Chinese, since he had a good job and a good life. But I could tell that the resentment was there, beneath the surface. I didn't know how much I could pry, so I went about it slowly.

"Do you have family in Turkmenistan?" I asked.

"Yes, a lot of family."

Now came the difficult part. The question I wanted to ask was, *when East Turkistan was a country, was it joined with Turkmenistan?* And I wanted to ask if families had been ripped apart by the land grabs made by China and the Soviet Union. I also wanted to know if he was still pissed off about this.

"Why did you move to China? Don't you miss your family?"

"We did not move," he said, with a candor that I did not expect. "But now the border runs between us."

"Do you see them often?" I asked.

He had a sly grin on his face, looked over both shoulders, and said, "All the time."

This was a situation which the Chinese called *a security concern* and which many liberals in the west called *a fabrication.* I believed the answer was somewhere in between. The Chinese claimed that they needed heavy security in Xinjiang because the Uyghur were sneaking out, having meetings with terrorist groups, and then returning with weapons and plans for revolution. Because the Chinese were able to sell this bill of goods to The US government, Xinjiang was now part of the war on terror, and China is justified in anything they wanted to do there.

Liberals in the West said that it was preposterous to believe that anyone could sneak out of China, or that the Uyghur could be part of international terror organizations. They said that Uyghur missed the call to *Jihad* (religious war) because they had no communication with Muslims in other countries.

Friends in the know have told me that because, to the eyes of a Chinese soldier on border station duty, a Uyghur can look like a Pakistani, there are Uyghur who sneak out on delivery trucks. Or, they switch documents with foreign-born Turkic people or with Uyghur who have exit permit. They say that there is some chance that Chinese Uyghur were fighting in Afghanistan. In his book about the Taliban, Robert Caplan said that he personally saw Chinese Muslims fighting in Afghanistan. He said that they looked and spoke Chinese. This would suggest, however, that he was talking about the other group of Muslims in China, who come from Kunming and Yunnan. They are ethnic Chinese, who converted to Muslim centuries ago. If they, being so far away and looking nothing like Arab or Turkic people, were able to get out, then I had to believe Uyghur also got out.

In Taiwan we would occasionally hear about bombings, by Uyghur terrorists, directed against Chinese targets in Xinjiang. Most journalists believed that China suppressed the majority of these stories, and that for every one we heard about, five were not reported. They also believed that the casualty counts were much higher than official sources had reported. While the Chinese needed to publish some data about Uyghur militarism to justify their war on terror, they would be afraid of losing face if the world knew that large numbers of Uyghur had snuck across the border, or that there were significant incidences of violence.

For myself, I tend to be pro-Uyghur. So, I am biased. But I will say, that at no time in Xinjiang did I get the impression that the Uyghur were anti-American or anti-Western. They seemed to be either ambivalent or perhaps angry that the West wasn't helping them. They all did know, however, about the various Gulf Wars, 9-11, and the war in Iraq. They all mentioned Saddam Hussein, and Ben Laden at least several times. Often they would just sort of throw their hands up in defeat, and ask, "Why does the US kill Muslim people?" Their question seemed not to be motivated by anger, but more out of non-comprehension. They would inevitably say something like "You do such good things everywhere else. Why do you kill Muslims?"

After dinner I went back to my room, but, predictably, I couldn't find the key lady. I found the fourth floor key lady who told me, "The third floor key lady will let you in to your room."

"But I can't find her."

"Just go down there and wait for her. She will come along eventually."

Eventually? I didn't want to go to my room eventually. I wanted to go to my room ten minutes ago.

On my eighth round trip, down the hall and back, I found the key ring lying on a desk. I could not believe that they had left the keys lying out like that. I opened my room, but considered opening every room on the floor. I wanted to brush my teeth and take another shower before going to use the Internet. I knew that my family would be worried. I wanted to get a message out before curfew, but I wasn't sure if the curfew was at eleven or midnight.

Of course, there was no water in my room. Fuming mad, I marched right into the main dinning room and brushed my teeth in front of all the guests. I was hoping to create a scene. But this being China, half the guests were picking their noses while they ate. The other half cleared their lungs and spit luggies on the marble floor.

When I found the key girl, I complained that she had left the keys lying on the desk.

"No, I didn't," she protested. "I always keep them with me."

"Then how did I get them?"

"I always keep them with me," she maintained.

I returned the keys to her, and told her that there was no water in my room.

"Yes there is."

"No, there isn't. Come look."

I lead the girl back to my room, and pointed at the bathroom. She fiddled with the knobs, but no water came out. Eventually she gave up, and disappeared into the hallway, leaving the door open behind her.

In the West, if the girl left to get the fixit guy, she would have said, "I will go get the maintenance man. Wait here. It should just be a minute." Then she would have closed the door when she left. But of course, this would never happen in China.

I waited several minutes, with a sneaking suspicion that I was waiting in vein. I found the girl cleaning a room down the hall.

"What about my shower?" I asked.

She had a frustrated look on her face, and said, "You see it doesn't work." As if this explained everything.

"I am aware of the fact that the shower doesn't work. That is why I told you it doesn't work. Do you remember me telling you? But you didn't believe me. So, now that we both agree that my shower doesn't work, what are you prepared to do about it?"

"It's no problem," she assured me. "You have already brushed your teeth."

"Yes, but I want to take a shower."

"You already had one."

"In civilized countries people bath more often."

"Use the shower on the fourth floor," she suggested. "They have water. And many of the rooms are vacant."

"But my room is on the third floor. And besides, I don't have the keys for the fourth floor rooms."

"The girl probably left the key on the desk."

"But how will I know which rooms are empty?"

"Just use any of them. Most of the people are eating dinner now anyway."

I demanded that the custodian come and check my room. While I was waiting for him I noticed that my fan didn't work either, a man pushed my door open and entered without knocking. Neither did he introduce himself.

"The fan is not working," I said.

"Yes, it is."

"No, it's not."

"How do you know?"

"Because when I switch it on, nothing happens."

He looked at me suspiciously.

"You must be doing it wrong."

"I'm not doing it wrong. How long has it been broken? And, why didn't you fix it before? I imagine the last guests to stay here also tried to use it."

He ignored me, and set about dismantling the fan. In the end he determined that the plug was broken.

"Will you attach a new plug?" I asked.

He looked at me like I had said the stupidest thing in the world.

"No need for that, he said."

To my horror, he took his pocketknife, which was his only tool other than a heavily rusted, ten-pound masonry hammer, and cut off the damaged plug. He used the blade to split the cord. Then, separating the two wires, he stripped them back about three inches, exposing the copper ends beneath. He stuck the naked wire into the wall socket, and there was a bright flash of light as current arched through the air, making a popping sound and creating smoke with the smell of ozone.

He looked at me triumphantly, as if to say, *See how easy it was for me?*

There was a light wisp of thick black smoke jetting out of the wall socket.

"On second thought, I'd rather not use the fan," I said. "You can go ahead and unplug it."

"Don't be crazy. It is hot in here. You can't sleep without a fan."

"Please unplug the fan instantly," I said, changing my voice to one of command. There was another bright arch and an even louder *POP!* as he jerked the wires free. He had obviously burned his hand, because he was shaking it in the air. He had just about made it out the door, when I stopped him.

"What about my shower?"

"You already had a shower."

"I know. But I want to have another one."

"Why?"

"That's got nothing to do with you."

"Wait here. I'll be right back," he said, turning to go.

"No! Fix the shower first." I didn't want him disappearing.

Annoyed, he went to work on my shower. It was getting late, so I went out in search of an internet cafe. Along the way, I ate another meal and several ice creams. I also drank a number of liters of water and several sodas.

The Internet cafe was just like in Taiwan, except that the kids were Uyghur. They hung out for hours playing video games, mostly first person shooter games. Instead of Taiwanese pop music, however, they were listing to cover versions of American pop, sung in Uyghur language. They actually had an entire album of Ricky Martin, the Uyghur version. I particularly liked their rendition of *uno, dos tres, tres pasos por adelante Maria.*

Since translators for any language, other than English, are rare in China, I would assume that translators for Spanish to Uyghur must be non-existent. Probably, had I understood the Uyghur text, the meaning would have been nothing like the original. I wondered if the kids even understood that these songs were originally from the United States. In Taiwan, they didn't know that Ricky Martin, Christina Aquilera, Santana, and the other Spanglish pop stars sang part of the lyrics in Spanish. Even seeing the text written out, they would just assume that it was English.

When I returned, I knew full well that the shower would not be working. I pulled open the tap, and sure enough, it was as dry as the desert I had left behind.

The bed was lumpy and painful. People came and went in the hallway all night. At least once someone opened my room door, prompting me to block it with a chair and to sleep with my fighting stick, as I had done before. Without a fan the room was hot and stuffy. I missed the cool breeze and the airy comfort of sleeping out in the desert, under the stars. In the morning, once again, there was no shower. I brushed my teeth with my drinking water, and marched into the dinning room, ready for a fight.

The owner was there, acting all innocent, as Chinese bosses do. He first denied that my shower didn't work. Next, he said that it was the fault of his staff. He apologized, and said, "I was at home when this happened. What could I possibly do?"

"You could refund half my money. I suggested."

He pretended not to understand what I had said, which I had been expecting. My normal procedure in these situations would be to become, loud, threatening, and even violent.

To my surprise, his wife got up, walked to the register behind the bar, and handed me my money. It was the first responsible action I had ever seen committed by any person of authority in China.

The owner looked to his wife, askance.

"I want us to continue to be friends," she said.

Suddenly, the owner changed his tact. "Yes, we must always be friends. I am sorry that you had such a bad stay."

They offered me breakfast, but I refused, just wishing to be rid of them.

For all of the issues I had in the hotel, psychologically, it had been a break. Although I probably could have gone on for several more days, now that I had stopped, my body thought the trip was over. Everything began to break down. My knee didn't want to bend. My butt was on fire. My hands wouldn't open and close properly. And all of my muscles were in complete rebellion.

The final forty-five kilometers to Kashgar were interminable. The final day was also the day of the most intense sun I had experienced during the whole trip. I actually heard the cytoplasm in my brain boiling.

Far off to the right, across an expanse of about one kilometer of barren desert, I thought that I could see a huge, cool lake glistening in the sun. I wanted nothing more than to run over and jump in. Assuming I was just hallucinating, I tried to ignore it. But, no matter how long I rode, this lake kept beckoning me.

What appeared to be one kilometer of straight line distance across rolling sand dunes could easily have been ten times that distance once I actually started walking. That would mean the walk to the river would have taken hours. It would have required several liters of water. And what if I was wrong? What if there was no river there? The thing about a mirage is that it makes you walk and walk. It always appears to be just a little it further. Then, before you know it, you are lost or dead.

In the end, I took some advice from an old *paisano*. In the diaries of his travels, Marco Polo had warned that all along the Silk Road the traveler would hear voices and spirits beckoning him to abandon the path, and walk into the desert. He would then lose his way and die of thirst.

Rejecting the promise of swimming in a cool lake, probably full of ice cream, I twisted my wayward handlebars back into position, more or less, and continued to Kashgar.

My bike began rattling apart. First the carriage jumped off of the rear axle. Then the handlebars came loose, and began rotating like a crazy radar antenna. I had to hold them at a forty-five degree angle just to go in a straight line. This meant that about every third revolution of the pedals, I would bang my knee into them.

I stopped at a work camp, and one of the men helped me tighten the handlebars. They held for a while, but then started spinning again.

To motivate myself, I sang a modified version of a song I stole from the rock group, The Clash. *Rock the Kashgar. Rock the Kashgar.*

The narrow road I had been on lead into what looked like the beginnings of a small city. I asked a woman if this was Kashgar. She started laughing at me. I had asked in Chinese. *Je she Kashi ma*? But, since this failed, I asked again using the Uyghur name for Kashgar, which is nearly the same as English. *Kashgah? Kashgah?* But she just continued laughing, and turned her back on me. I asked several more people, none of whom seemed to understand Chinese, or have the presence of mind to answer me.

At a major intersection, I turned west and followed a four-lane road through the center of a large town. If this was Kashgar, I couldn't believe that there had been no sign. If it wasn't Kashgar, this was no small oasis. It was a good-sized town. Why wasn't it on the map? The street was lined on both sides with businesses, everything from small restaurants to cell phone shops and department stores. At a kiosk I drank several bottles of water and soda. The owner made a seat available for me under a shaded awning, so I took a break. Some old men sat at the only table, talking as if they had been there all day, or more probably, as if they were there every day. Getting up my courage, I asked the men who had been staring at me the whole time if they spoke Chinese. One man answered in the affirmative. He told me that Kashgar was still seven kilometers away. He also told me there was a bicycle repair place across the street.

The bicycle repairman was wearing typical, Arab style clothing – a long white robe, and a white skullcap. He didn't look at me. Neither did he answer when I talked to him. Instead, he just grabbed my bicycle away from me, roughly. He tried the pedals. Satisfied, he tried the brakes. Then, determining that the problem was the handlebars, he straightened them out, and tightened them up. He disappeared into his house, and I was left, standing on the street, not knowing if he was coming back or if he wanted me to give him money. I tried knocking and shouting at the door. Finally, he stuck his head out a window, and in an angry tone motioned for me to go away.

Once again, I was rolling down beautiful, tree lined streets, with attractive, freestanding houses. This was one of the only places in China where I had seen people take such care and such pride in their homes. The houses were all well painted and well turned out. Many had decorative shutters and tiled roofs. I was surprised to see so many flower gardens on the manicured lawns.

Two young boys, probably about twelve years old, rode up beside me on their bicycles, singing a Taiwanese pop song, which I recognized in spite of the Uyghur lyrics. They were really funny kids, keeping pace with me, very curious about my bike and all the things in it. They kept doing impressive rodeo tricks for my entertainment. One boy kicked his legs back and rode with his chest on the saddle. He looked like superman, flying through the air. The other boy jumped up and put his knee on the saddle, then balanced with his arms out like a bird. Maybe they had escaped from a circus, I thought. I remembered being a little kid and wanting to run away and join the circus. Now I wondered if little kids who grew up in the circus dreamed of running away and going to school.

We played chase and tag, with my too heavy bike keeping up as well as possible. When one boy came too close, pretending he was going to jump onto my cycle, I pulled out one of my Kung Fu sticks and pretended to shove it into his front spokes. We had a good laugh, counteracting my frustration from the people earlier in the day, who couldn't tell me whether or not this was Kashgar. Maybe these two boys were the official welcoming committee for the town. If they weren't, they should have been.

The way to Kashgar lead onto a rural road, which ran through a heavily forested stretch of land. It was good to see trees again and to get some shade. But, it also made me sad. This meant that the desert portion of my trip would soon be at an end, and that my trip itself would soon be over.

When I went to Shaolin, I had promised myself that it would be the start of a life of adventure, with each successive adventure better than the one before. Coming to Xinjiang was the fulfillment of that promise. And, for the last several weeks of planning, reading, researching, and eventually riding, I didn't have to think about the next adventure. I didn't have to think of anything. When you are on a trip, you live as you would have lived in nature. Hunger determines your meal times. And that could be ten times a day, or it could be once. Convention doesn't exist, only your body. The same goes for sleep. If I wanted to sleep four hours in the middle of the day, I could do it.

But soon the trip would be over. I would return to Taiwan, and probably take a teaching job for a while. Convention and social norms would be forced on me again. I would deal with such issues as renting videos, using an ATM, watching cable. And every day I lived in domesticity would be another day that I got weaker. It would also be another day that civilization strengthened its grip on me. Maybe it wouldn't let go next time. Now I had to worry again about what my next adventure would be, where, and when.

The road snaked around wooded curves. In the distance, far below, I could see a town, which I thought must be Kashgar. At a roadside stand, I stopped and bought a melon. Some small Uyghur boys stared longingly at the Uyghur ice cream the salesman was preparing. I bought two bowls of the ice-cold creamy treat and gave them to the boys. The happiness in their eyes made me smile. I ate that melon very slowly, knowing that it might be my last melon as an explorer. When I am on a trip, and I stop to eat, I feel like I am taking on fuel. When I am home, I feel like I am taking on fat. Out here I was someone special. The Uyghur and the Chinese alike wanted to hear my tale. And they all treated me like a hero. Back in the world, I would jut be another Joe.

With remorse, I realized that I had eaten the last of my melon. Like a convict, finishing his last meal, I knew I could prolong the inevitable no more. I mounted up, and pedaled slowly.

The road took me down a steep hill, and ended at the main street of Kashgar. I was surprised at how big the city was. I was picturing an intimate oasis town, which it probably had been when Sven Hedin was there. But today, Kashgar was a big, communist city with a strange mix of concrete block buildings and gaudy mosques. The streets were alive with people. There was commerce and activity everywhere. In the Arabic tradition, the Uyghur were great traders. There were peddlers on every corner, selling all manner of goods, from pots and pans to horses. Being on the streets of Kashgar, smelling the smells, and hearing the din made me hungry to visit Central Asia, the former Soviet Republics, Pakistan, and Marekesh.

I had laughed at people who were shocked that I had no specific plan of action once I reached Kashgar. But now that I was here, I realized that they probably had a point. I had no idea of where to go. Pedaling up and down the noisy streets, I saw the old and the new, the Chinese and the Turkic. The many three wheeled bicycles and the occasional horse drawn wagon looked out of place in the midst of so many banks and cell phone stores. Searching for a place to stay, I finally decided on The People's Hotel. It was a good Communist name, which I thought would help me slowly assimilate back into the world of the Chinese.

Taxis and private cars drove up the red carpet on the circular driveway, where a tuxedoed concierge greeted the passengers and took their luggage. For a lark, I considered leaving my rickshaw with the valet, handing him a twenty, and saying, "Park it next to a Rolls." Instead, I decided to chain my rickshaw to the flagpole out front and walk in.

There is always a bit of suspicion about people who arrive at a hotel on foot. If they didn't have money for carfare, how would they pay for their room? There is always quite a bit of suspicion about shabbily dressed people, who smell badly, who arrive at a hotel on foot, tracking half the desert with them. I had a cloud of dust following behind me, like the Pigpen character on Charlie Brown.

"Can I take your bag, sir?" asked the tuxedoed concierge, already touching the shoulder strap with one of his manicured hands.

"I got it," I said, pulling away from him.

The clerks eyed me a little suspiciously, but seeing that I had cash, they gave me a room.

"Can I take your luggage?" asked a bellhop, who weighed less than my carry on bag.

"I'm afraid you would fall over," I said. Truthfully, I was embarrassed at how dirty my bags were. I didn't want him to soil his uniform. The bellboy was required by the management, ultimately by the Party, to offer two more times. He seemed relieved when I insisted on carrying my own baggage.

"There is just one thing," I said, preparing to utter the phrase I had been looking forward to my whole trip, and one I would probably never get to say again. "What should I do with my rickshaw?"

"Your what?" he asked, assuming he had misheard me.

"My rickshaw."

"I'm sorry, I don't speak English."

"I am speaking Chinese," I assured him. "I rode across the desert on a three wheeled bicycle, and I have it chained to a post out front."

The bellboy did what people in low positions always do in China when they have a problem. He called the next higher up. The desk clerk, an impeccably turned out and bright looking young lady listened to my tale, and then called her superior. Eventually I had all the clerks, the bellboy, the concierge, the manager, the cook, the baker, and the candlestick maker listening to me tell and retell my story of crossing the desert. They all insisted on following me outside to see my bike. One look at my sand-encrusted vehicle, and they knew that the story was true.

"We can't risk letting it get stolen in the car park," said the manager. He had the concierge and the bellboy carry my bike into the hotel. They dragged it through the lobby, scuffing the marble floor, and chained it right to the banister of the spiral staircase. Talk about putting a silk hat on a pig. The only thing in that hotel that looked more out of place than me was my filthy rickshaw.

Several guests came over, and soon guests and staff alike were asking me all sorts of questions.

"Where did you sleep?"

"What did you eat?"

"How did you carry water?"

"Weren't you scared?"

"Where are your friends?"

"Did you get lost?"

"Why aren't you married?"

"Where did you buy the rickshaw?"

"Was the Iraq invasion really necessary?"

"Does your bottom hurt?"

"How much did you pay for the rickshaw?"

When I told them I had paid 360 RMB, they all agreed that I had been cheated.

When I felt I had been polite long enough, I excused myself to my room, where I took the longest, hottest shower ever. Only minutes after leaving the road, I was already plagued with the question of *What now?*

When I was working in Guangdong, there wasn't a lot of evening entertainment, so I used to treat my best Chinese friend, Ah Bing, to an evening at the hair salon. There, a haircut, plus a one-hour full body massage, clothed, was 36 RMB.

After my shower, I went down to the hair salon, and had the girl wash my hair for me. Nearly two weeks of constantly wearing a baseball cap, and of not washing, called for professional intervention. When I first walked in to the shop, the girl spoke Uyghur to me. Even after we switched to Chinese, her friend wouldn't talk to me. She only spoke Chinese to the one washing my hair, as if I needed a translator. She asked if I was Uyghur or foreign. I told them I was foreign, but somehow they didn't believe me, probably because I looked poor. The girl told me I was the first foreigner she had ever seen.

In China going to the hairdresser is like a night out. First, she started by putting me in a reclining chair and placing hot towel, after hot towel on my face. Next, she washed my hair, just with hot water. After that, she shampooed it. Then she scratched my scalp for about twenty minutes with her fingernails. Then she massaged my forehead and the back of my neck with the soapy water dripping down from my skull. She washed my hair again with hot water, and dried my head with a towel. Next, she put the towel over my back, and gave me a massage on my neck, back, and shoulders for about twenty minutes. The fee for all of this was 20 RMB (less than two dollars).

After a week in the desert, I needed a full body massage, but in the hotel it was 150 RMB, which seemed expensive to me at the time. And, the massage was probably not a real massage. Most likely, it was a prostitution service. In China it was often very difficult to find a real massage.

As long as I was in Kashgar, I figured I should go look at something. The only things that I really wanted to see were Chingiba, which, as I mentioned, had been the pivotal location of so much of The Great Game, and John's Caf, which was supposed to be the modern equivalent of Chingiba, a place where foreigners could gather, eat some Western food, get information, or arrange trips. Supposedly, for enough money, John – a notoriously dodgy fellow – could arrange anything.

I had planed to have dinner at Chingiba, and then go to John's for coffee. Hopefully, I would meet some interesting travelers, and we could sit around and tell stories all night. Chingiba was the biggest disappointment of my life. When the taxi dropped me off, I didn't believe the driver that the tasteless, concrete monstrosity before me was the former residence of Consul and Lady McCartny. In the books I had read, Chingiba had been described as a large Victorian home, a small bit of England, resettled in East Turkistan, complete with English garden. Instead, Chingiba was a shabbily maintained, neon-fronted tourist trap. Touts hanging around out front offered services from photography, to black market money exchange – and in very bad English. There were vendors selling stupid, plastic souvenirs of China and the Uyghur people. Among them were such must have items as a *matruchka*, those Russian dolls where there is a big doll on the outside, and inside there is a smaller doll, and inside that is still a smaller doll... But this one, in keeping with the Chinese tradition, was a doll of Chairman Mao. There was a Sun Yat Sen alarm clock, which played Communist marching music. And, I think I even saw a snow globe of the Forbidden City.

For months I had imagined what it would feel like to pass through the great gates into that historic place. But now, you have to *run* through to avoid the mob of street hustlers. It reminded me more of a heavily-touristed street corner in Cancun. In the compound there was one building, marked *Western Restaurant*. And another, marked in English, *Chinese Restaurant*. Apparently, they had forgotten to build a Uyghur restaurant.

Inside wasn't much better. Not only was there nothing distinctively English about the place, there was also nothing distinguishably Uyghur or Chinese. It was just like any other, personalityless hotel, servicing the first world visitors from all over the globe. Among the Dutch and Japanese businessmen engaged in boring conversations, speaking global English, the only remnant of the old history was the spiral staircase which lead to the restaurant. Still hungry, and not yet ready to dash all hopes, I mounted the stairs, thinking, perhaps, I could meet some nice people while I was eating some roast beef or whatever they ate in those cold islands where Bill Clinton didn't inhale.

Once again I was disappointed. The dining room looked like any other hotel dinning room in any hotel in China, except worse. The menu entries only offered Chinese food, written in very poor English. Not one item on the menu cost less than what I figured as my food budget for two days. The lights were out, and yet the seventy-five staff members, who had nothing to do, didn't understand why I chose not to eat, as the soul guest in the one hundred-person dining room.

I couldn't get out of Chingiba fast enough. Dodging the taxis, I chose to walk, losing myself in the Uyghur part of town, where the streets were teeming with activity. In a crowded restaurant, I ate my last Uyghur meal. It was skewered goat's meat, served with soup and bread. The bill was around 25 RMB. It was a little more expensive than out in the desert, but still cheap. I couldn't believe that Westerners at Chingiba would be dining on institutionalized Chinese food and paying 250 RMB for the meal.

Where Chingiba had been the biggest disappointment of my life, John's Caf was the second biggest. It was barely a cafe at all. The inside was closed. There were only two tables outside on the cement porch, under an awning. The first ten menu items I asked for were unavailable. In the end, I settled on chocolate mouse. The consistency was somewhere between rubber and an old tire, with pockets of mouse powder which hadn't been mixed properly. I took two bites and gave up. The coffee, however, was excellent.

At the other table, there was a bored looking German lady and an older Canadian guy. The Canadian, Dave, was the one interesting person I met in Kashgar. He was a geology professor, specializing in snow and avalanches, come to China to do a skiing exploration of a mountain. The story was so interesting, that unfortunately, I forgot to ask him if he had been in the Kun Lun, Lop Nor, or Tien Shan mountains.

Dave told me that he had climbed mountains all over the world, including the Andees, Alaska, Canada, the Alps, and the Himalayas. He and his teammates had just completed a seven thousand foot climb to the top of a mountain, which took three weeks, because they had to acclimatize, to avoid altitude sickness. It only took them an hour and a half to ski back down. He was fifty-seven years old.

We discussed the fact that he and his team were obviously fit and experienced. But, in today's world of adventure tourism, guides are being offered large sums of money to take people, who have no business mountain climbing, to the tops of dangerous peaks. Even if a guide had a conscience, and turned the client away, someone else would take him. In the end, the business was about taking people up the mountain. What business willingly turned away clients?

Dave told me that when he was at the base camp, a Belgian guide came down the mountain, nearly dead. He pretty much collapsed within sight of the camp, and several climbers went out to take his pack from him, and help him get back in. The guide said that he had been hired to take two clients to the top of the mountain. Unfortunately, the clients were so unfit, that it had taken them three weeks just to reach base camp. The guide cancelled the contract and sent the clients back to Kashgar. Not wanting to waste a free trip to base camp, the guide decided to make a solo ascent of the mountain, Alpine style. He made it to the top in record time, but was nearly dead by the time he reached the bottom.

These were the kinds of stories I lived for. One story like that made my trip to John's Sucky Caf worthwhile. Now I had one more dream to take with me when I went to bed.

The German lady had a nice, humorous way about her. After I had told them my story, she laughed and said, "Here I have one who climbs mountains. And over there I have one who rides a bicycle in the desert. I am just a tourist, on vacation. I am the only normal one here."

The John's reputation had been so built up on the Internet that I thought we would have met a hundred interesting tourists, and my story would be the least adventurous of all. I had expected to see camels tied up out front, and meet a Swede and a New Zealander who had ridden all the way from Peshawar. The woman who was running John's that day told me that normally, in the summer time, John's was like this. But because of SARS, no foreigners had been allowed into Xinjiang in six months. In fact, John's wasn't even officially reopened yet. I gave her, and John, the benefit of the doubt. I promised that if I came back next summer, to ride a camel from Hotan to Aksu, I would stop into John's for a coffee.

The German lady refused to pay for her food. "This place is so bad!" she said. "And yet it is so famous. Could you imagine what the not famous places are like?"

I had originally planned to spend two nights in Kashgar. But seeing that Kashgar had no redeeming qualities, I left at five o'clock the next morning. The clerk at the checkout desk didn't know me, so he didn't ask about the bike I left behind. Before finding a taxi, I took one long, sad look at the rickshaw that had served me so faithfully during what had been the coolest adventure of my life. It looked sad and lonely there, chained to the stairs. But, it also looked tired. Maybe after they realized I wasn't coming back, someone would give it a good home, and not work it as hard as I had.

Leaving my bike behind and stepping into a taxi, I knew the transformation was complete. I was no longer an explorer. I had left the ranks of Sven Hedin and Marco Polo behind, and just became another guy from Brooklyn, trying to get home.

Once again, I couldn't get a sleeper for the interminably long train ride back to Urumchi. At least this time I had a seat. The trip took thirty hours, but it felt like a hundred.

I was running so low on money, now, that I wasn't even sure how I was getting back to Hong Kong. The one smart move I had made was that I had only bought a one-way ticket to Xian. This left me free to fly out from any airport in China, or to take the train. Just a few hours on the train, however, convinced me that there was no way I could stand the several days-long journey to Hong Kong, no matter how cheap it was. I was going to have to take a gamble at Urumchi, and see if I had enough money for a plane ticket back to Hong Kong. I knew that this would cause me to incur taxi costs, which would eat into my dwindling funds and might result in me only finding out that I couldn't afford the ticket to Hong Kong, but I had to try it.

My seat on the train was at a four-person table,

which I shared with three men from Henan, part of a party of at least twenty in our car alone, returning from months of work in the desert. The first thing that struck me about the men, besides their used up, overworked, prematurely aged appearance, was that not one of them had more than a single piece of hand luggage. Actually this is not strictly true. They each carried a huge sack full of melons to eat on the trip. But other than the melons, all of the gear and clothing they had needed for nearly a year away from home was contained in a single bag, which fit in the overhead compartment.

The men all marveled at the size of my rucksack. The color alone was beautiful, and the fabric was one they didn't see often. Their small bags were all made of cloth, and couldn't possibly have contained more than a single change of clothes and a few changes of underwear. It is amazing how simply we can live if necessity dictates. Or said another way, it is amazing how much we, in the West, think we need to survive and be comfortable.

These men had already been on the train for at least one day, and when we got to Urumchi, they would still have several days to go. I couldn't imagine living like this. The train lacked even a single ounce of amenity or comfort. The seats did not recline, neither were they big enough for my huge body. I felt bad for my neighbor, as I was pushing him out into the aisle.

During the long journey, the men didn't read. They talked, but only periodically. Occasionally, they played cards. Mostly, they just sat and stared. I could not believe the countless hours that these men sat, quietly staring off into space. If you live a simple life, are your thoughts simpler? Do you expect less diversion? For me, I read constantly on that trip, finishing one huge book and starting another. The big event was when one of them would break out a watermelon. This was Christmas and Mardi Gras, all rolled into one. The men all carried knives on their belts, some as large as a good hunting knife, which they used to butcher the melons. But it didn't take much imagination to believe that they could also have used these knives to fight, if their honor were at question.

With beaming faces, they cut up the melon, sharing with everyone in their general vicinity, myself included. Then the chatter would start. Blades flashed. Juice dripped. Men joked and asked me questions. Happily, they chewed the red meat of the fruit, sucking the rind, and spitting the seeds directly on the floor. The Chinese are prodigious spitters to begin with. You never ever want to come in contact with a floor in China. But in a train full of workers, armed with a seemingly endless supply of watermelons, the debris would pile up several inches thick.

Friends had told me that since the SARS epidemic, the Chinese government had been encouraging people to adopt cleaner habits. Supposedly, the spiting on public trains has been eliminated in the rest of China. One friend said that you could tell the Chinese took SARS seriously. Because now, they all wash their hands when they go to the bathroom. The joke is, they wash them *before* they go, not *after*. Someone else said, "I thought it would have taken more than a few hundred deaths to get the Chinese to wash their hands."

Every hour, on the dot, an extremely aggressive cleaning woman came through, sweeping the floor. Her diligence was commendable. Even if you were dead asleep she would wake you and sweep under your feet. She scolded the Uyghur and Henan men, even hitting them with her broom, ordering them to move their feet. Her Nazi-like zeal disturbed my rest.

But I couldn't imagine how filthy the train would have been if she hadn't been so insistent.

The cleaning woman was not the only person yelling at the Uyghur and Henan men. The train police came through with almost the same regularity, demanding to see everyone's papers. Once again, I had to question this practice. When we started we were already several hundred kilometers from the Pakistani border. As the train progressed, it seemed less and less likely that there were illegal immigrants aboard. This is, of course, making the assumption that Pakistanis would want to immigrate illegally to China. Often it was several hours between stops, and yet the documents would be checked multiple times. If no new people had gotten on, then wouldn't the assumption be that everyone had already been checked?

I didn't get it.

The policeman, of course, was Chinese. He shouted at the Henan men, treating them like small children. He knew where they had been and why. But it wasn't enough for him that they had just spent months in the desert, working like animals, separated from their families. Now, he had to harass them as well. At times, he came through ordering the Henan men to close all of the windows in the stifling heat. At other times he came through ordering them to open the windows. Once he came through while a melon was being eaten. The men were all out of their seats, singing and laughing. He ordered them to sit down and be quiet. It was like when you had your friends over, when you were a teenager, and your parents came home early.

Not that I expected special treatment, but being the only foreigner on the train, I thought he would have remembered having checked me an hour earlier. And yet, every time, I had to show him my passport. And every time, I had to explain to him which of the words was my name and which was my entry and departure date. Each time he would look at the photo suspiciously, and hold it up to my face. By about the fifth time I felt like saying, "Yup, still me."

When the men felt comfortable enough to talk to me, they asked me all of the usual questions of *Where are you from?* and the like. But then they started in with the game of *How much was this? How much was that?* They started with my boots. Apparently, these construction workers really liked my boots for some reason. The pity about the boots was that I was planning to throw them away as soon as I reached Hong Kong. They were just too dirty and smelly to be salvageable. If I had had other shoes to put on, I would have been glad to give my boots away on the train.

The next thing they asked about was my Walkman. They stared at it curiously. Then one of the men asked if he could touch it. Hesitantly, he reached out a single finger. There was a moment of expectation, where all of the men waited for something traumatic to happen, like laser beams shooting out. When they did not, everyone breathed easier. They were asking if the Walkman played movies and if it had Internet. I swapped the CD for one of Jay, my favorite Taiwanese pop singer, and let the men listen. They huddled around, passing the earphones from man to man, squealing with delight. They asked to look at the CDs and seemed to have only a vague concept of what they were.

I must point out that this behavior was not typical of all of China. Beijing, Shanghai, Guangjo, and many other areas of China are nearly as developed as Hong Kong now. Even in small cities in Guangdong, where many people still can't afford a Walkman, they would know what one was. But these men were from Henan, which is still quite underdeveloped. And, to make matters worse, they had been living in the Taklamakan

Desert, which is not exactly on the cutting edge of new technology.

When they asked how much a Walkman cost, I cringed. It was US$60 dollars, probably a month's salary for them. Next, they wanted to know how much a CD cost. I didn't tell them, but the CDs probably cost an average of US$12 each. I had fifty CDs in my bag. That was nearly a year's salary. I put the CD player away, not wanting to offend them. I went back to reading. Suddenly, the face of the man across the table from me blanched.

"Is this the price tag?" he asked, pointing at the label on the back of the book.

"Yes."

"This says 190. That's one hundred and ninety what?"

"Hong Kong dollars," I answered. A Hong Kong dollar was worth slightly more than one RMB. So, if he was earning 500 RMB a month, my book had cost almost two weeks salary. I had about seven books in my pack.

I considered putting my book away. But then what would I do, stare off into space like the rest of them? My brain was screaming – *I'm sorry! I'm sorry you are poor! I'm sorry your country only decided to join the 20th Century five years ago. I'm sorry you have to travel thousands of miles from home and earn in a month what many of my friends spend for dinner in Hong Kong.* I felt guilt, impotence, and anger all at once. I suddenly felt anger toward these decent men for forcing me to have to think. The least charitable voice in my head was saying, *Well, if you didn't want to live like this, you shouldn't have voted for Mao.*

I used the phrase *This is China* once more. And I realized that there is no phrase less accurate in the world. What is China? Is it the new economy in Shanghai? Is it the old communist government in Beijing? Is it the uneducated masses, who eat rice three times a day in Henan? Is it the Uyghur people, tending their goats out in the desert? Is it the Shaolin Temple? Is it the soldiers I saw, bristling with weapons, zealously raiding a building in Aksu? Was it my gentle friends in Guangdong, who like to go to karaoke and laugh and sing? And now both Hong Kong and Portuguese Macao were part of China. So the question was, what is China? And, would I ever know?

At the next stop, the policeman was replaced by a younger cop. He was extremely friendly, which made him very annoying. I think he just wanted to practice his English, so he came and talked to me constantly, making my skin crawl. He would smile and talk softly to me one moment, then turn, and scream at one of the Henan men the next.

Because he wanted to practice English, I didn't let him know that I could speak Chinese. Although speaking Chinese probably would have facilitated communication, he would have lost face. He gave me a stern warning – *There are many bad people on this train. So be careful of your parents.*

It took me a minute to understand what he was saying, and I had to suppress a laugh. He meant, *Keep an eye on your baggage.* I thought it better not point out his error. But I couldn't resist taking the piss out of him. I assured him in my sternest voice.

"Thank you so much. And I can assure you, I will watch out for my parents."

"Yes, if they are stolen, please let me know."

"I will. The moment my parents go missing I will call you."

"If you would like, I could lock your parents up in the vault."

"That won't be necessary just now."

A man, who looked like a Uyghur ,kept staring at me on the train. He was staying in another car, but each time he passed through our car, he gave me a long look. I actually thought we were going to have a problem. By chance, I was getting up to check out the restaurant car just as he was walking by. Finally, when I could stand his constant gaze no longer, he spoke.

"I know you," he said. "You came to my village a few days ago on a bicycle."

"That was probably me," I laughed, but not quite convinced. I thought maybe he had overheard me telling someone else about my trip.

"You took our pictures, everyone in the village."

This was astounding. It was strange to know that when I got back to Hong Kong, I would have a photo of this guy. He invited me to share some beer with him in the restaurant car. I accepted, but immediately regretted his company. He was big, fat, imposing, and already drunk. As much as the thought of a beer seemed appealing to me, in practice, it was all I could do to swallow one small glass of the foul tasting liquid.

The man told me that he was *kiird zu ren*, which in my mind, I had translated as Kurd. Later, back in Hong Kong, when I finally met Bill, the explorer who had encouraged me to go on this trip, he explained that the man was probably a *Kiird*. This is another Turkic group, following the religion of Islam, which has lived in the desert for centuries. If I am not mistaken, Polo even mentions them in his book. The man told me that the Kiird are a small minority of only forty thousand people in Xinjiang. An interesting incidence of cross assimilation was that the Kiird man and the Kazak girl I had met both spoke Uyghur in addition to their own language and Chinese. I imagined that being labeled as non-Chinese, and Muslim, all of the smaller minority groups had to learn to live within a Uyghur dominated sub-society.

I managed to extricate myself from my new Kiird friend, and spent most of the rest of the trip talking to some college students on their way home for school holidays. In the States college students are normally full of hope, and much of their discussion revolves around their plans for the future. In China, I didn't get the impression that there were many plans for the future. The kids would graduate with their degree in English, and then be assigned, by the government, to teach at a school which may be anywhere in China. In China, one would often hear of workers, both professional and laborers alike, who would first be granted leave, to see their families, after many years.

In Urumchi I had the taxi driver take me to the travel agent. The two choices she gave me were flying to Guangjo, and then on to Hong Kong that night. Or, flying to Guangdong, arriving at midnight, and catching the train to Hong Kong the next morning. The first option was more than I could afford. The second option only left me a few hundred Hong Kong dollars to spare. I prayed that I would get a cheap room in Guangjo, or else I would be stranded. One of the fun things about running out of money in mainland China was that even if a friend or family member put money into my Taiwanese bank account, it was not one hundred percent guaranteed that I could use my Taiwanese ATM card. I chose the second option, as the lesser of two evils.

The only memorable thing about the airport in Urumchi was that everyone was Chinese. I guessed the Uyghur couldn't afford to fly.

I arrived in Guangjo, only to find that there was a conference in town, and all of the hotels were booked. After my long trip through the desert, and the interminable train ride, followed by the airplane, I was now so exhausted I could barely stand. It was barely forty-eight hours since I had finished pedaling to Kashgar. In the end, I bribed a hotel clerk to let me take a nap for a few hours in an unused room. In the morning I took the super luxury, double-decker train to Hong Kong. There is something magic about crossing the border into Kowloon. A wave of relief always washes over me, and I think, *I made it. I am safe.* After an hour on the subway and a little walking, I made it to the guest house which is my home in Hong Kong. The owner and his family were all waiting for me and handed me a big stack of mail when I arrived. My room was ready. The girls took my dirty laundry from me before I lay down on the bed. I slept for nearly twenty-four hours.

I woke up with severe stomach cramps, fever, and chills. I spent the next eighteen hours in bed, before holding a brief meeting with friends. Barely two days after arriving in Hong Kong, and still less than five days out of the desert, I was on a plane for Kaohsiung, Taiwan, my home. From the time I went to Shaolin temple, then was stuck in Hong Kong because of SARS, and then to Guangdong, and then to the Taklamakan Desert, I had been away from home for nearly six months. I was anxious to get back.

On the short flight, I had a chance to reflect on my journey. No one had given me a medal when I got to Kashgar. Neither was there a ticker tape parade waiting for me in Hong Kong. The trip was just over. But the journey continued.

In the last few years, one of my major heroes has been Dan Eldin. He was the youngest correspondent ever to work for Reuters, and the man personally responsible for calling world attention to the troubles in Somalia. When Dan was stoned to death in Mogadishu, he was only 22 years old. His diaries and his life story have since been published and have become an inspiration for me. In his journal, he had written a phrase, which I have taken to heart. *Mission statement: Safari as a way of life.* Even the title of his book, *The Journey is the Destination* inspired me.

Life is not about achievements or rewards. It is about having an interesting path along the way. My goal is to keep going and going. I want to ride a bicycle around the island of Formosa. I want to live in a Muay Thai temple in Thailand. I want to be the first American to cross the interior of the Taklamakan Desert from south to north, with a camel. I want to go to Burma and Cambodia, and live and experience, and meet people, and learn, and learn, and write and write and write.

I left my rickshaw in Kashgar, but I am still on the move.

Debauchery
and
Decadence
on the
Elephant Polo Trail

When you ride an elephant, you feel like Hemingway. When you play elephant polo, you feel like F. Scott Fitzgerald. When you take a break from elephant polo, sit in the air-conditioned comfort of a silk tent, and have the native boys bring you a Chivas on the rocks, you feel like Hemingway again. And when you attend the huge formal galas, dancing under the stars, with titled Lords and Ladies, you feel like Fitzgerald again. And when you shoot a lion from the back of an elephant, and get in a boxing ring with Gertrude Stein, you feel like Hemingway.

Basically, when you play elephant polo, you go back and forth between feeling like Hemingway and feeling like Fitzgerald. It is an advanced form of schizophrenia, which by the end of the week, had me debating if I should drink myself nearly to death and then shoot myself, like Hemingway, or drink myself nearly to death and then drive off a cliff in France, with my crazy poet wife, Zelda, as Fitzgerald had.

It was a toss-up between the two. But either way, I knew that elephant polo wasn't going to end well for me.

I had been in Phnom Penh, minding my own business, making kung fu movies, working as a freelance spy, and failing to write a book about the very illusive Khmer kung fu. It was so hard to get any reliable information on this dubious martial art that I was beginning to believe that it was the Yeti, the Sasquatch, of fighting systems. After four months of work, I had only one page of text, which I had stolen from the desk of a government sports minister. It was written in Khmer, so for all I know it was his grocery list. I purposely didn't allow anyone to translate it, however, as the myth that this paper held the secret to the lost martial art of the ancients kept me going.

It was a hot, humid, corruption-riddled August morning, when government sensors, disguised as mototaxi drivers, watched me reading my e-mail. Becoming disappointed at the lack of state secrets or revolutionary texts I was passing to foreign nationals, they decided to pick up some extra money, driving foreign tourists to the killing fields, which left me alone to read in peace. The first message was from Hardy, my editor, back in Chiang Mai, which simply read, "Elephant Polo is a Go." Through a very distant fog, I remembered one of my final meetings with Hardy before leaving Thailand. He had just done me a lifesaving favor, and I had asked if there was any way to repay him. His answer was, "In September there is an elephant polo tournament for the King's birthday. I have always wanted to be in the tournament, but I think I am a bit too old and unfit now."

Hardy had always been a great friend to me. In addition to buying stories and photos from me, he also handled all of my mail and banking while I was off in the jungles of Burma, doing stories. He also arranged much of my sponsorship. The only reason I was able to do some of my best stories was because Hardy knew people who could finance my trips. And, what personal compromises he had to make or what favors he owed as a result, he never mentioned. He always just seemed so pleased to hear about my trips when I returned to Chiang Mai.

Although I never had the kind of relationship with another editor like the one I had with Hardy, I did enjoy good relationships and a good amount of support from a number of editors. In most cases they either hinted at the fact, or blatantly came out and told me, that they were living vicariously through my adventures. Hardy had told me long ago about the elephant polo tournament and how it had always been his dream to play. He said that he would call favors, even if I would go play in his stead. "If I could put a team together and arrange the sponsorship, would you go?" he asked.

I was on my way to Phnom Penh the next day and had no idea what lay ahead or how long I would be gone. "Of course," I said, absently. The likelihood that Hardy could raise the tens of thousands of dollars necessary was so remote, that I agreed, thinking I would never hear about this elephant madness again. But here it was, in my inbox, saying I would have to be in Thailand in less than a week. I had a life in Phnom Penh, all be it a dog's life, but how could anyone expect me to drop everything and run off like that? I had a job. I had a movie opening in a few days, and I was a big star. I had a house. I had friends.

But then the thought of another adventure put the rest of my life in Phnom Penh in perspective. I hated my job, working for the Cambodian government, defending Cambodia from Nuclear Biological and Chemical terrorist attacks. I had been looking for a way to quit the cloak and dagger world of Communist Party politics, and a sudden and unexplained trip abroad might just create the suspicion I would need to get myself fired.

I had long ago realized that my movie was absolute crap, and thought it might not be a bad idea to miss the launch. They say any publicity is good publicity. But I think it might be better to remain unknown than to be known for the worst movie ever made.

My house was a guest house, where the family treated me like their son. They invited me to their parties, expected me to marry their daughter, came to watch my boxing matches, and over-charged me for every service they provided for me. Further, I knew that some of the drivers I used had been paid off to keep an eye on me. Communism had ended in Cambodia, but a repressive, one-party government was very much alive, and I worked for them.

My Khmer friends were excellent, and they kept me laughing and helped me with the language. But, I paid for everything we did together and gave them generous tips for the slightest favor. At the end of the day, I knew they were paid friends, but they were the only friends.

In the words of Herman Melville's Ishmael, from *Moby Dick, Having little or no money in my purse, and nothing particular to interest me on shore, I thought I would sail about a little and see the watery part of the world.*

Or, in my own words, *Seeing that my life in Cambodia was nothing, I went back to Thailand.*

As excited as I was about riding around on elephants and playing Gatsby, rubbing shoulders with Europe's rich, I was a little nervous about the gig. First of all, money is always an issue. As a freelance journalist, I live a hand-to-mouth existence which is quite stressful. Normally, my journalism takes me to the jungles of Thailand, where it is a bit easier to live with nothing. But heading to that most decadent of all sports, elephant polo, a sport invented for people who felt horse polo was too inexpensive, I knew there would be a much greater opportunity to spend money.

I was curious to find out how Hardy was funding this little outing. But the sponsorship turned out to be another source of mystery and confusion. Hardy had arranged for a company, called *Kuoni*, to pay the entrance fee for me and my team. Right off the bat, I didn't have a team. So, Hardy arranged for two other journalists from his competitor's magazine, *City Beat Chiang Mai*, to join me. I was a little baffled as to why Kuoni had been unable to send players of their own. I just assumed that they would send a representative to meet us. In the eight days that we spent at the tournament, we only met one Kuoni employee, who was there by accident, and who had no knowledge of our existence.

City Beat and I had a long running relationship. Over a period of seven months, they had rejected every story I submitted to them. On the eighth month, they blocked my e-mail. This made coordinating with my two teammates a bit difficult. As a special concession to Hardy, *City Beat* had agreed to pay my hotel cost for the week. Hardy was sending me a small allowance with the *City Beat* crew, and we hoped that with that, and a bit of luck, I would somehow survive.

One nice thing was that the agreement Hardy had with Kuoni was that they would get as much press as possible. This meant that he wanted me to resell the story as many times as I could. This would give me a nice financial boost, but not for a period of months, when the magazines would finally decide to pay me.

My instructions were to take a bus from Bangkok to Huahin and rendezvous with my two counterparts at the cheap guest house where we would be quartered. I was very nervous about meeting Christopher, the team leader, as he had been the one who sent me my final rejection before *City Beat* had blocked my e-mail. I found Christopher and his colleague, Einarr, at the bar. They were both younger than me by about ten years, but didn't look much fitter than Hardy; and I was wishing, once again, that he had been able to make it.

The first few minutes with my teammates were a

bit tense. What they knew of me personally they had obviously learned from the Internet. From magazine articles appearing in obscure publications on four continents, they had assumed that I would be some half-crazed jungle man, who was violent, uncouth, and relentlessly self-promoting.

"How are you doing?" I said, extending my hand. It was a bit tacky from a tree I had just climbed to steal a coconut, in a fit of hunger. "I'm boxing on Thursday. I hope you guys will cover my match and run the story in your magazine."

One of the magazine editors I worked for had come up with the idea of having me box in a benefit for the elephants as a way of getting me more publicity. The hope was that with the entire international press corps present, that they would rush to cover an event where one of their own was stepping into a boxing ring.

"I heard something about that," said Christopher, a British guy with a good education and a Sting haircut, circa 1982. "Would you like a Beer?"

Christopher and Einarr were both champion drinkers. But since I was fighting later in the week, I thought it better to abstain.

"No, just water," I answered.

The look on Christopher's face said that if I had agreed to beer, I would have made a major step in bonding with my new teammates. Instead, I was as far away as someone who had been rejected eight times, and then had his e-mail blocked.

"We read your story about caving, in the *Huahin News*," said Einarr, opening the magazine to the appropriate page. The problem with publishing in Thailand was that I never got to see my stories in Phnom Penh. "It's pretty funny," he added with his crazy Nordic accent.

Einarr was from the Faro Islands, a semi-autono-

154■

mous landmass off the coast of Scotland, but somehow belonging to Denmark. At twenty-eight years old, he was the youngest of us, but proved to be the most uptight. His chopped off haircut made me refer to him as "the Dutch Boy" for the rest of the tournament.

"Sorry, I don't speak freaky-deaky Dutch," I said, quoting Doctor Evil, in his conversation with Goldmember.

"You mean Faroese," he corrected.

"Oh, Faroese? No, that language I speak fluently. But Dutch has always been my Waterloo."

"That's in Belgium," corrected Einarr, giving himself away.

"I know. I was being ironical."

I had been with them only two minutes, and already I felt that my teammates hated me. "What did you do before *City Beat*?" I asked Christopher.

"I am a poet," he said.

"Wow!" I actually was impressed. It takes a phenomenal mind to create poetry. It is a genre I have never attempted to read, much less write. "And have you published any books?"

"No, I do performance poetry," he explained. He apparently had founded the authors open reading night in Chiang Mai.

"So, you are an ex-poet who has became a journalist," I summed up.

"I am not a former poet," said Christopher, a little bit heated. "I *still* am a poet."

At this point, I added to my list of worries that I would not be getting along with my teammates. By calling him a *former* poet, I had insulted him so much that I should have just asked him if I could use some of his writing to wipe my bottom.

In spite of my lack of finesse in dealing with people, Christopher would turn out to be my best friend during the elephant polo debacle. And what's more, he would prove himself to be the ultimate peacemaker and smooth talker. He could diffuse any situation which I caused by my total lack of decorum. In this instance, he simply let my insults slide and suggested that we sit down and discus our situation.

Staying in a cheap guest house bummed us out because not only would we have to tell the other players that we were poor, but we would also miss out on so many of the events and dinners and things. How would it look, when all the other rich players were sitting down to a meal together, and we three pulled out paper bags with sandwiches?

"The most pressing issue is transportation cost," began Christopher, unfolding a large map. "The Bekhenshire, the big fancy expensive resort hosting the tournament, is here, about five kilometers north of town. The polo grounds are here, on an army base, about five kilometers south of town. And we are here, stuck in the middle. I just checked with the hotel guy, and he said it will cost us about one hundred baht each way to the polo grounds, and the same each way to the hotel."

Mornings would start at the polo grounds, so one hundred baht. Then we'd need to go to the hotel, which from the polo grounds could be two hundred baht. And then we'd need to come home again at night, so, a grand total of three hundred baht. And this was assuming that we never came back to the hotel to take a shower or change clothes. It also didn't give us an opportunity to eat lunch or dinner, since meals at the big hotel probably ran about one thousand baht each.

Hardy had sent along a per diem for me of two

thousand baht for the week. I knew that Hardy didn't have a lot of money, and that sending even this small sum may have meant that he wasn't going to be able to eat. So, I was grateful for the help. But it looked like the money would be absorbed by taxi fare and meals by the end of the second day. I only had five hundred baht of my own, as I was waiting for a paycheck from the *Bangkok Post* to come in.

"Apparently, there is a press dinner tomorrow night, and we should be able to go to that one for free," added Christopher.

"How do you know about this?" I asked.

"It's in the press kit they left in your room. Did you read it?"

"I meant to, but it had a lot of words and things."

Christopher let my feeble excuse slip by him without any reaction. Man! I love the English. At those great schools over there, not only do they learn perfect diction, but they get the emotions sucked right out of them. If Christopher had been Italian, he'd have called me a *Momo* already. I was willing to bet he didn't even know the word Momo.

"Momo!" I yelled.

"Pardon?"

Yeah, I loved the English.

"We have a few hours to practice on the elephants tomorrow morning. Then we play in our first match-up the following day."

"How do you know this?" I asked, amazed.

"The press kit has a schedule of events."

"I was saving that to read on the bus on the way home," I answered.

"I don't guess I should bother to ask you if you went on the elephant polo website and read up on the rules?" asked Christopher.

"No, I don't think you should ask me that. Just always make the assumption that I didn't bother to inform myself about anything."

"But don't you care?" asked Einarr, in an accusatory voice.

"Not particularly. I am here for the story. And the quality of the story will be the same, win or lose. In fact, the story is usually funnier if you don't know anything."

"But I don't want to go out there on an elephant, with my mallet and pith helmet, and look silly," said Einarr.

"Then you've probably chosen the wrong sport," said Christopher.

Einarr let Christopher's comment slide and continued his attack on me. "Do you even have an opinion on how we should play?" he asked.

"Yes, my opinion is that Christopher should be leader, because he knows how to read, and he owns the only map."

"You have one too," said Christopher. "It's in..."

"...the press kit?" I asked, finishing his sentence. "This is why you should be in charge."

"You can only hold the mallet with one hand," blurted out Einarr, trying to impress us with his knowledge of the rules.

"There's a mallet?" I asked.

I honestly didn't know. People had asked me before going to Thailand if the elephants hit the ball with their trunk, or if you used a mallet. To give us an edge, I had gone out and purchased some pharmaceuticals. I figured if the opponent's elephant had a Viagra caught in his trunk, he'd be too stiff to play. But now I saw the drugs wouldn't be necessary. I was trying to think of a good distraction to slip them into Einarr's drink, just for a laugh, when Christopher suggested we go grab some dinner at the night market.

"Do you have horse polo experience?" I asked Christopher. He had such a great accent, I just assumed he had spent his youth playing cricket in between sets of horse polo, while his servants tended to the garden.

"None, you?"

"No, we didn't play much polo in Brooklyn. There was a horse in front of the barbershop. But you had to put a nickel in it if you wanted a ride. And, who had a nickel?"

"I've played pony polo in the Faro Islands," said Einarr.

I hated the way he kept mentioning the Faro Islands, as if that were a real place.

"You can be our leader on the polo grounds," I said. "And Christopher could be our leader everywhere else."

Another reason why I wanted Christopher as leader was because his cell phone worked. My account was too low to make calls, and Einarr's phone only responded to oral commands shouted in Dutch.

Although he had the press kit, Christopher still wasn't sure what, precisely, we were expected to do the next morning. He made several calls, and eventually reached Rachel, the public relations director for Robert Stockton.

"Who is Robert Stockton?" I asked.

"Robert Stockton is the richest *farang* (foreigner) in Thailand," they both answered in disbelief.

"Ah, ha, and this concerns us because..."

"He also owns the largest chain of luxury hotels in Thailand, including the Bekhenshire."

The blank look on my face prompted him to continue his explanation. "The Bekhenshire are the hotel hosting this event."

Now it all made sense.

"So why didn't you call Rachel earlier?" I asked. "My room is too small. And there is no button on the phone to order up a massage."

"Sorry, I am only doing the best I can," answered Christopher. "Anyway, she was shocked that we were staying in this dump."

"So am I."

"She said that there are suites reserved for us at the Bekhenshire."

"Is that because we are big important journalists?" I asked.

"No, it is because Robert Stockton will come and be the forth man on our team," answered Christopher.

"Oh great!" yelled Einarr. "What if he doesn't know how to play?"

"Then he could buy us a win," I said.

Guests of Robert Stockton! That made us very happy. We did a dance of friendship and joy through the stalls of the night market. Had this been a musical, swarms of children would have gathered behind us, doing a jig of their own. Food vendors would have joined us in a song, keeping time, banging on their pots and pans – or is it woks and pans?

Now that we found out about our all-expense-paid spa vacation, we were psyched. And the bonding started.

"So, this Robert guy is pretty rich then?" I asked.

"Dude, he is the richest farang in Thailand," repeated Einarr.

"When we meet him, we should be, like, *Hey, rich guy, how much money do you have in your wallet right now?*" said Christopher.

"I know how we can win this thing," I said.

"How?"

"Two words – pea...nuts. We could fill our pockets with peanuts and cut holes in the bottom. Then, while we are riding around, we could shake our legs and make the peanuts fall out. Everyone knows how elephants love peanuts. So when the opponents' elephants are too busy loading up on free grub, we could score.

"Peanuts is one word," pointed out Einarr.

"You're right," I agreed. "That was clearly the flaw in my plan."

At a pet shop, I asked if they sold rubber mice. "If Saturday morning cartoons haven't lied to us, then we all know how afraid elephants are of mice. It could give us a psychological advantage."

"But wouldn't our elephants also be afraid of mice?" pointed out Christopher.

"OK, no mice. But what about amphetamines? We could buy a hundred pounds, or kilos, or trashcans-full of *yaba* (amphetamine), and slip it to the elephants."

"Ours or theirs?" asked Christopher.

"I see your point. An elephant hopped up on yaba would be pretty fast. But on the other hand, he might be a little hard to control."

"Exactly. And until we work this one out, I would suggest against buying truckloads of illegal substances. Besides, what if they have doping tests? Our elephants could get disqualified."

At a stall which sold martial arts weapons, I loaded up a rucksack with brass knuckles, slingshots, darts, and throwing stars.

"To give us an edge," I suggested, lifting the heavy clanking sack onto my shoulder.

"I think people may notice," said Einarr.

I threw the sack back down on the table, which flipped over. "You don't like any of my ideas! So what are we supposed to do? Go out there and play fair and square?"

"That would be within the rules," he agreed.

The next morning, while we were at the bar drinking coffee, a very attractive Thai girl, in a solid black Kuoni t-shirt, accosted us.

"You are late," she said.

"Late for what?" asked Einarr.

"And you are?" asked Christopher.

"Not married," I answered, seeing that she wasn't wearing a wedding ring.

"Yes," she answered, according to perfect Thai decorum. They are trained, from birth, never to reveal any information about anything. I guess it could be an advantage if they were captured during a war. But during peacetime, it is just damned annoying.

"We go now?" she said, obviously expecting us to follow.

"Who are you?" I asked again.

"Bea," she answered, and again expected us to follow.

"No, he means are you from Kuoni?" asked Christopher.

Blank stare.

"Your shirt says Kuoni on it," I prompted, hoping this would awaken sleeping beauty.

"Yes, shirt," she said, as if I had reminded her of something.

She opened her shopping bag and handed us each two *Team Kuoni* polo shirts. They were all extra large, which upset me, because I wanted a medium one which would show off my muscles in the photos. Next, she handed us each a photo ID card, which we were to wear around our necks all week to gain access to the polo grounds. One would think the polo shirts would have clued the security guards that we were players.

But they may have been slow-witted relatives of Bea.

Christopher and Einarr had both mentioned that they had had to submit photos of themselves in advance. But since I had never been asked for a photo, I expected my ID to be blank.

To my chagrin, the photo on my ID badge was clearly taken from the website of the kung fu film I had just finished in Cambodia. I played a bad guy, with a three-day beard, bulging muscles, a mean face, and a very bad attitude.

"Nice photo," complimented Christopher.

"Thanks."

"We go!" insisted Bea.

"I'm not going anywhere!" I protested. "I still don't know who you are."

Bea looked confused. "I tell you already, you are late."

"I don't think she means us harm," assessed Christopher. "And she is cute. And she does have a Kuoni t-shirt..."

"And I guess that excuses her rudeness in not telling us who she is or where she is from?" I knew that sometimes there were language barriers, but there was no excuse for bad manners.

"You can see her breasts," pointed out Einarr.

"That does excuse bad manners," I agreed. "OK, I'll go. But let the record show I went under duress."

"Take your luggage," commanded Bea.

We loaded our gear and stretched out in the back of a chauffer-driven, air-conditioned minivan, with the words *Team Kuoni* painted on the side.

"Bea, may I ask where we are going?" asked Christopher.

"Yes, going," she agreed.

"No, I mean where are we going?" he repeated.

"Not going?" she asked, confused. "But you must go."

"Look, Kafka!" I shouted, losing my patience. "Where are you taking us? It's a simple question."

"You don't want to go to hotel?" she asked.

"I didn't say that! Are you taking us to the hotel?"

Bea looked worried, and told the driver in quick Thai to stop.

"We go somewhere else?" she asked.

"You are a Momo!" I said.

"The hotel would be lovely," interjected Christopher.

And Christopher was right. The hotel was lovely. The Bekhenshire was a tremendous complex of luxury rooms, surrounded by manicured tropical gardens, centered around a tremendous swimming pool, the temperature of bath water. A bar floated in the middle of the pool, dispensing frozen drinks with little umbrellas on them.

As we pulled into the palm tree lined drive, Bea turned to us and said, "Naomi Campbell stay hotel. And also Cindy Crawford."

"Wow! Did you hear that? We are going to meet Naomi Campbell and Cindy Crawford," shouted Einarr.

"No we aren't," I said. "Thais don't use grammar. She said, 'They stay hotel.' This could mean they were here last year, or they are coming next year. It could mean anything."

"Are they here now?" asked Einarr.

"Yes," answered Bea.

"No, you see. She said they are here now."

Einarr had only been in the country a few months and hadn't figured out Thai English yet.

"They always say, 'Yes,' even when they have no clue what you are saying. In fact the one phrase I have never heard in my seven months in Thailand is, 'I'm sorry, I didn't understand that,'" I explained.

Einarr was about to protest when I said, "Watch this." Then to Bea I said, "Bea, are they at the hotel now?"

"Yes."

"And do they know I am coming?"

"Yes."

Christopher was usually too nice to aid me in torturing our translator by speaking English, but this time he couldn't resist.

"And are they staying in our rooms?" he asked.

"Yes."

"Is Einarr handsome?"

"Yes."

"You see, Einarr, she doesn't understand a word of English," I concluded.

The first view of the hotel, when I stepped out of the van, was so overwhelming that I didn't see the Thai guy making a grab for my backpack. Luckily, before he could get a solid grip, I spun out of his reach and brought my hands up ready for a fight. Suddenly, Thailand was just like Cambodia. Even in a wealthy resort, they couldn't ensure the guests' safety from common thieves.

"Can I take your bag, sir?" asked the very gay bellhop in an extremely meek and effeminate voice.

Normally, one should apologize at this point. Instead, I played it off. "You can't touch this bag. It contains dinosaur embryos, the last of their kind. They are keenly tuned to my body frequency and temperature. The slightest change could send them into decay."

"Decay?"

"Yes, but they don't like to go down alone. I can tell you that. The gasses they emit, when they spontaneously decompose, would kill us all. We'd begin projectile vomiting, and eventually bleed to death through the pores of our skin."

The bellhop gave me a long look. I wasn't sure if it was me or the dinosaurs, but he was clearly frightened of something.

"You can take my bag," suggested Christopher.

The boy gave the bag a long hesitant look, then gingerly picked it up and carried it to the reception desk.

The receptionist gave us a registration form, which had a space for credit card number.

While Einarr, who had no money worries as a result of his huge socialist stipend from the Swedish government, gladly wrote out his credit card information, Christopher and I simultaneously bent down to tie our shoelaces so we could have a whispered conference away from prying eyes. We both came to the same conclusion. Namely, we had been told that we had reservations at the hotel. But no one had told us that the rooms were complimentary. And if the rooms were complimentary, why did they require a credit card number?

"Maybe it's just a formality," suggested Christopher.

"OK, then let's give them your credit card number for both of us," I said.

"What if they actually expect us to pay for this? Seven nights in this place has got to cost..."

"At least fifty bucks," I suggested, picking a number that was out of my price range.

"Maybe I should try to reach Rachel."

"Good idea. But for me there is no worry as your boss, Stena, said she would pay for me." My editor, Hardy, had arranged the sponsorship for all of us. He was an enigmatic character. No one knew what he had done in England or why he was in Thailand. Some said that he was hiding out. Others said that he had killed a man. Still others suggested that he did origami and composed Russian operas in his spare time. Who knew? But somehow, he had managed to have this company, Kuoni, pay for Christopher, Einarr, and me. In return, Stena was to pay for my hotel.

"That was when we were staying in the cheap place," said Christopher. "I don't think Stena is going to pay for this place."

"Oh sure, now that I am moving up in the world, I lose all of my friends."

"Stena's not made of money."

"Stena's jealous. That's the problem."

"Is everything all right down there?" asked the confident voice of a New Zealand businesswoman. Her ankles were the first things we saw. But when we got to her face, we realized how silly we must have looked.

"Fine thanks. And you?" I asked.

"Rachel?" asked Christopher, more than a little embarrassed.

"Yes, I just stopped by to see if you got checked in OK. But then I saw you on the floor..."

"It *is* marble!" I exclaimed, slapping the hard stone with the palm of my hand.

"I told you," said Christopher as we stood up. "You owe me a beer."

Rachel looked at the forms the staff had expected us to fill out and frowned.

"No! These are all wrong. These gentlemen should have complimentary rooms and breakfast."

I was beginning to like Rachel.

"You guys go get settled in. Then you have to go to the polo grounds for elephant practice," she explained. "Have you met your ambassador?" she asked.

"Who?"

"Bea, she is your Kuoni team ambassador and translator. Anything you need, you tell Bea. And if you want to go anywhere, the Kuoni driver is waiting to take you."

We were thanking Rachel when she received a call from *Sports Illustrated*. They were shooting the swimsuit issue in the hotel and needed some help on the set.

"If *Sports Illustrated* needs anything, we are right here," hollered Christopher, as she ran off.

We later heard the story about how the *Sports illustrated* shoot nearly ended the entire elephant polo tournament. Although elephant polo is a strange game invented by very rich *farangs* (foreigners) basically because they had already done everything else, it has a uniquely Thai flavor. For one thing, elephants are considered holy animals in Thai Buddhism. Further more, all of the elephants in Thailand officially belong to the king. There is no joking when it comes to elephants. The elephants must be blessed before the game can begin. There was a huge ceremony where monks and old mahouts came to anoint the mighty beasts with holy water and adorn their necks with leis made of fresh flowers. After the blessing ceremony, there was an elephant parade, followed by an elephant banquet where the animals were allowed to eat all they wanted – not that anyone could have stopped them. It is quite a site to see an elephant lift an entire pineapple into his mouth, or to chew up a whole coconut. According to the caretakers, an elephant eats eighty kilograms of food per day.

Women must be properly attired when they ride the elephants. The police almost closed down the weeklong tournament because one of the *Sports Illustrated* swimsuit models posed on an elephant, wearing a skimpy bikini. As a foreigner you should respect the elephants. Besides, you'd probably want to stay on the good side of any animal that size, anyway, especially since he eats *your* body weight each day.

Rachel was a smart lady, and she knew her job. Some apologies, combined with a large payoff to the police, plus a few phone calls to high-up people, from other high-up people, and the tournament was back in business.

On the way to our stadium-sized rooms, I asked Christopher, "Do you know exactly how much these rooms cost?"

"No, I don't."

"Neither do I. Ya know why? Because they are *free*, that's why. I am staying in the fanciest place in the world, and it's *free*."

I took a quick shower and was watching cable when my teammates stopped by to tell me it was time to go to the polo grounds.

"Why is your door open with the air conditioning on?" asked Einarr, sounding like my mother.

"Because it is free!" I said, still not used to the concept.

"But it is bad for the environment," he chastised.

"How could that be? All that cold air will counter global warming."

"What is that all over your floor?" asked Christopher, meaning the towels.

"I took a shower."

"How many towels did you use?"

"Five."

"But what about the environment?" asked Einarr, mimicking a broken record.

≡169

"I got two words for that, *free*! Besides, there won't be a global shortage of towels soon. I just called room service and ordered some more."

"Let me guess," began Christopher. "Because they are free."

"That's the spirit."

In front of the hotel, the bell cap asked if we needed a taxi.

"No thank you, my good man, we have a *private* minivan," I answered.

Inside the van, we each stretched out across our own seat, lounging to our fullest in air-conditioned comfort.

I glanced out the window at a taxi carrying some foreign tourists.

"Ah yes, the poor people. I almost can't remember when we used to travel like that." Then I told them the truth. "Normally on my adventure trips, I sleep in caves, out in the desert, and travel by canoe or bicycle. So I can't get over this trip."

"Yeah, it is better than my apartment in Chiang Mai," said Einarr.

"I feel like a Rock Star. Maybe we should trash our rooms," I suggested.

Christopher had been laughing at all of my jokes, but now he looked a little annoyed. "They are picking up the tab for all of this. And that's great. But we shouldn't act so needy. We should act like we are used to this kind of treatment."

"Christopher's right," said Einarr. He was good at adopting whatever the prevalent opinion was.

"I'm not used to this. I mean what are they thinking, putting us in a minivan? Where is my limo? Bea! Bea! Where is my limo?"

"That is exactly the behavior I am talking about," said Christopher. "That's no way to get in good with our hosts."

"Yes," she answered from the front seat.

"You see, Christopher, even Bea agrees with me."

When we arrived at the polo grounds and got our first look at the other players, it became apparent that my humor was just a smoke screen to compensate for feelings of inadequacy. And it wasn't the size of my external male genitalia that was the root of the problem. It was the fact that everyone else, on each of the other fourteen teams, belonged in the elephant polo crowd. They were all impossibly wealthy gentlemen and ladies, mostly from Britain, who not only stayed in hotels like the Bekhenshire on a regular basis, but also played horse polo, flying around the world with their favorite steeds. They were people of leisure, who owned multiple homes, the smallest of which was a mansion, and the largest of which was a castle. They chose to spend several months of the year in Thailand, but listening in on their conversations, I heard them mention all of the right locations: Monaco, Andorra, Lake Lucerne, and The Canary Islands.

Where I was wearing cheap Khaki pants from the street market in Phnom Penh, all the other players had extremely expensive, bright white polo trousers, specially fitted to their wealthy posteriors. Where I had my usual expedition boots, which I had purchased at a discount store in Taiwan, they all wore knee high boots of the finest leather.

There was a British army team, made up of retired officers, who were characters right out of a movie. They told stories about their glory days, fighting her Majesty's battles for colonial expansion. I listened in on one man who sounded exactly like Commander McBrag, on the *Rocky and Bullwinkle Show*.

"After the regimental coolies ran off, I found myself surrounded by fifty wogs. But luckily, superior breeding and discipline paid off, and armed only with a sharpened mango, I managed to fight my way out, and summon the Maharaja's household cavalry."

Being the only American, I felt that I had to constantly imitate a British accent. With the exception of Dick Van Dyke in the film *Mary Poppins*, who did what has universally been called the worst British accent ever in a film, Americans tend to imitate the RP British accent (*Received Pronunciation*) which is taught at swanky schools, such as Oxford and Cambridge. This is considered, by Brits, to be the most posh of accents. It is also one of the rarest non-regional accents, as RP is spoken by only five percent of the British population. Careful not to enunciate or convey any emotion at all, I mumbled, "I say, Christopher, do you believe the elephants are restless today? One of the blighters came through my mosquito netting during the night."

"You do realize you sound exactly like Dick Vandyke?" asked Christopher.

"Sorry."

"Chim, chimney, chimney, chim, chim, cheroo..." he sang. "It's completely preposterous for an American to imitate a British accent in the first place. But second of all, the only Brits who actually have that accent are here."

As we made our way across the grounds, someone pointed out Sir Giles Tupentop, the founder of elephant polo. Giles was a Lord – an actual, titled British nobility. He was taller than me. He was richer, clearly better educated, and he actually knew how to play polo. But the fundamental difference between Giles and me, the one that really set us apart, was his hat. Where I was wearing a smelly old pith helmet, which I got out of the bin of free loaners, Giles had a fitted pith helmet from the famous haberdashery in Knights Bridge, the fashionable shopping district in London.

"I say, Antonio, might I have a word with you?" began Giles. The light reflecting off of his highly polished riding boots was blinding. I put on my sunglasses to protect my retinas.

"You can have anything you want, as long as you let me wear the hat," I answered.

"I understand that you are a boxer," he began, but continued before I could reply. "I did a bit of boxing myself. It was required in the army. I had one fight. Lost, you know. Never cared much for the sport after that."

I wasn't sure what I was supposed to do with this information. I smiled and was about to say something pleasant like, "Good for you." Or, perhaps, something more British, like, "Jolly good, Old Man." Or maybe, just a flippant, above-it-all one-word quip, such as "Rather."

Whenever someone like Giles – that is to say, someone with breeding and polish, someone who knows which fork to eat with – speaks to me, I feel exactly like a deer in headlights. I freeze up and revert to my own social etiquette, or lack there of. "Yes," I said, through my smile, hoping something intelligent would come next. It didn't.

Giles laughed in that way that cultured Brits do when something isn't actually funny. It was a single, explosive laugh, *HAAAA!* like a karate chop, after which, Giles walked away.

The press kit contained a rather gripping tale of how elephant polo came into being. But the theory I subscribe to is that the rich are bored, and that they invent unusual sports to entertain themselves – such as croquet, yachting, and sailing. Cricket is perhaps the greatest example of what happens when you have too much money and nothing to occupy your free time. A single game could last for three days, and end in a tie score. Any person of normal means would fall asleep in the interim. But the rich fortify themselves with expensive drinks and conversations related to other sports of the opulent, such as car racing and fox hunting.

Polo has all of the markings of a rich man's game. The horses cost hundreds of thousands of dollars. The players must be clad, head-to-toe, in an outfit which costs as much as most normal people earn in a year, but which can only be worn while playing. You tend to get strange looks if you show up at the food court at your local mall sporting a leather riding-whip and wearing a helmet and knee-high jackboots. If not for the skin-tight ridding britches, which clearly accentuate if you are circumcised or not, you could be the wayward soldier of some invading army. Instead, you just look like a leather-boy who got lost on the way to the Pride Parade.

Most people could afford the purchase of a horse and uniform, if they raided their retirement fund, and if they convinced their children to quit school and go to work in a poorly-lit garment factory in Indonesia. But, the expenses, which keep the sport exclusive, only begin there. Next, you have to actually play polo. Since my one bedroom flat is too small for polo, I found that I would have to join a polo club, which costs thousands of dollars per year. Next, since you don't just want to play in your hometown, you have to join the polo touring circuit. This entails paying entrance fees to the games and purchasing plane tickets, not only for yourself but for your steed as well. And finally, the tournaments, tremendous events played over a period of days, tend not to be sponsored by low-budget guest houses. Instead, they are hosted by luxury resorts, which cost big money.

This was my first experience with polo. And it wasn't even the regular, you-gotta-be-rich-to-play variety of polo. No, it was the granddaddy of all opulence – elephant polo. And yes, before you ask, elephant polo is played on the back of an elephant. The price tags associated with elephant polo are as massive as the elephants themselves. The only thing small about elephant polo is the circuit on which it is played. It includes only three countries: Thailand, Sri Lanka, and Nepal.

One of the reasons for elephant polo in Thailand was, that since logging has been declared illegal to save the trees, the elephants have become unemployed. New and creative ideas have to be thought up constantly to raise enough money to support them. Sideshows to the elephant polo tournament were the elephant art project, where elephants learn to paint. And the elephant orchestra, where elephants learn to play music.

Although it was interesting to watch elephants with paintbrushes, stroking away on canvas, I thought it would have been cool if spectators could have purchased white t-shirts, and then let the elephants paint on the shirts. Afterwards, they could have had a very unique souvenir, a t-shirt designed by elephants. And taking a cue from such sports as football, both American and regular, where you have painted fans, maybe the fans could have taken off the shirts and let the elephants paint them. And yellow journalists could have run the headline "Elephants Learn to Paint People in Thailand." The readers would buy the paper, thinking the elephants had learned to do portraits.

For a boy from Brooklyn, that first day on the polo grounds was a bit overwhelming. On my left was an elephant parade, where toothless old monks, shriveled like human prunes, were throwing out blessings. Dead ahead was the elephant percussion section and school of fine arts. And on my right, rich people were whacking a tiny ball with a long mallet from the backs of Hannibal's famed army tanks.

Wondering how this all came to be, I came up with this possible scenario. Two very old colonels, retired from His Majesty's Army in the colony of India, missed the excitement and glory days they once enjoyed – repressing native uprisings and quelling movements towards independence. I could see them sitting in a posh drawing room (who nowadays has a drawing room?). The room is decorated with the heads of exotic animals and tribal leaders who they killed in a place now referred to, nebulously as "The Colonies." They would be wearing red smoking jackets, with a distinct military cut and perhaps adorned with their medals and unit insignia. Their ascots would be held in place by a pin bearing the regimental crest. Both men would bare a large mustache, a monocle, and a pith helmet. The smell of oak would radiate from the fireplace, as the two men sipped their thousand-year old brandy from crystal snifters.

"Frazier, did I ever tell you about the time I was captured by the wogs and only managed to escape by fashioning a sailing boat from my underwear?" began Sir Albert Frederic Arthur George, the eighth Viscount of Mecklenburg-Strelitz and the Jersey Islands.

"Yes, I believe you have regaled me with that one on many an occasion," answered Sir Frazier Bowes-Lyon, Grand Duke of Hertfordshire and Connaughton, Earl of Strathmore and Kinghorne. "Ripping tale," he added, seeing the dejected look in his friend's eye.

"Have I ever told you of the time I was set adrift in the Horse Latitudes, and I was forced to eat my scribe?" asked Sir Albert, hopefully.

"And on the eighth day you hollowed out the regimental mascot and rowed to safety," said Sir Frazier, finishing the story.

"Yes, quite," said Sir Albert, slumping deeper into his eighteenth century armchair.

"Perhaps we need a bit of sport to liven up our conversation," suggested Sir Frazier.

"We could talk about fox hunting," said Sir Albert.

"It's been done."

"Polo?"

"Ho hum," yawned Sir Frazier, feigning boredom. "No, we need something truly exciting, something that brings back the excitement of our youth. And, of course, something so bloody expensive the rabble would never even consider mixing with us."

"Ah, yes, the rabble. Yes, wouldn't want them about, now would you? Dreadfully nice people, but then they haven't got two pennies to rub together."

"No, no, no. We wouldn't want the rabble to play our new sport. Also, this sport must have some connection with India."

"To India!" shouted Sir Frazier, raising his glass. When the glass was empty he asked, "What was it that made India so special?"

"We had servants and could order them to eat paste if we chose to," said Sir Albert, fondly remembering his past days of glory.

"Yes, there *was* that," agreed Sir Frazier. "But a paste eating contest sounds rather boring. What else was good about India, apart from the curries and boy brothels, I mean?"

"Do you remember the maharaja's household cavalry?" asked Sir Albert. "There is nothing so regal, so awe inspiring, so damned big as an elephant."

"Yes!" shouted Sir Frazier, springing from his chair. "Elephants! That's what we need, a bit of pachyderm sport would breathe some life into our stagnation."

And so it was that elephant polo was born.

Each team is composed of four members. No more than three members may play at a time, leaving one player in reserve. The game is divided into two chukkas, or halves, each lasting seven minutes, with a fifteen-minute break in between. The playing field is similar to a football pitch, with one goal post at either end. Just as in regular polo, the objective is to drive a small ball into the goal of the opponent, scoring one point. To drive the ball, the players use a mallet which, given the size of the elephants, is considerably larger than the one used in horse polo, generally two-and-a-half meters long.

The elephants are driven by *mahouts*, one of Thailand's ethnic minorities, whose job, for centuries immemorial, has been to handle elephants. The mahouts were small men, who perched, barefooted, on the neck of the elephant, steering the mighty beast with a combination of secret words and physical gestures. The mahouts used a metal hook to get the attention of the willful, if lazy, creatures, who apparently were less enthusiastic about elephant polo than the players were. The mahouts also kicked the backs of the elephant's ears to signal left and right hand turns. Since, I am told, an elephant's skin is several centimeters thick, one would have to believe that they hear, rather than feel, the blows.

Horse polo is one of the fastest and most exciting games in the world. But the fans of elephant polo, once they get over the initial excitement of seeing the elephants, will then be faced with one of the slowest games ever played. Elephants don't gallop. And, they don't turn on a time. The players have no control over the beasts. So, much of the skill of horse polo is missing. The one skill that remains quite similar, however, is *striking*. Elephant polo players must be as adept at swinging a mallet as their horse polo cousins. But, owing to their obscene length, the bamboo-handled mallets tend to bend if swung too hard. Bending shortens the mallet and results in the player missing the ball.

Another problem unique to elephant polo, is that the ball will often become lost under the elephants. At those most exciting moments, when all four players press in, close together, all swinging their extra long mallets, risking life and limb for the team, the ball suddenly disappears under one of the mammoth pachyderms. And as an ironic twist of fate, the spectators can all clearly see which elephant the ball is under, whereas the players cannot. As a player you begin hearing cries from all points of the stadium. "It's on the left!" followed by, "No, my left, not your left."

Often, even if a player manages to make the most brilliant shot of the day, a swing that would surly take the ball home, it is accidentally blocked by the impassable legs of an elephant, often from that players own team. Sometimes an elephant will step on the ball, burying it, impossibly, in the ground. In this instance, play must be suspended and a restart called. And of course, any sport which involves elephants will also involve elephant dung. According to the officials at the polo grounds, an elephant consumes eight kilograms of food per day. With six team elephants, and one referee elephant on the field, that gives the potential for five hundred sixty kilograms of excrement to be released, at will, by the elephants, often when the players are pressed close together in a scrum for the ball. Only the rich would require you to wear white pants in a game where there was any chance at all of being shat upon by an elephant.

On the practice field, I was amazed to find about thirty people riding around on elephants, hitting a ball with a long stick. I don't know what I expected to find. But it was still more than a little intimidating to see people riding on elephants, hitting a ball with a long stick.

"Are you gentlemen big elephant men?" asked the assistant, as he helped us suit up for our first foray on an elephant.

"Christopher is the expert," I said. "He was raised in an elephant preserve in Kenya, where his father worked as a naturalist. And Einarr has played pony polo."

"Well then you should be fine," he said.

To mount an elephant, you climbed to the top of a bamboo ladder and mounted from a little house, like a watchtower. Fears that I would have to control these wild beasts, and they were wild, evaporated when I found out about the mahouts. These men were almost a unique ethnic group, a tribe separate from mainstream Thais, whose job, for centuries has been to drive elephants.

After being strapped onto the massive beast, I was handed my mallet, which I really didn't want, as I wanted to keep both hands on the safety ropes. The mahout sat on the elephant's neck, and responded to commands in Thai, right, left, straight ahead...

It sounded easy enough, but elephants are scary

animals. They are unstoppable army tanks, like those walking battle ship vehicles in *The Empire Strikes Back*. The old joke kept reverberating in my head.

Question: Where does an eight ton elephant sleep? Answer: Anywhere he wants to.

With the heat and the commotion of so many people, and the camera flashes of a tremendous press corps, the elephants were noticeably skittish.

The previous year, an elephant had bolted, for no apparent reason, dragging the rider with him. Seeing that the elephant was heading for the potentially deadly foliage of the jungle, the mahout sprang clear, leaving the rider to his own fate. By some stroke of luck, the safety harness got caught on a tree, ripped off, and the rider fell clear. It took two days to recover the elephant.

Sir Giles, of all people, was covered with bruises from an elephant attack earlier in the week. The elephant, for reasons unknown even to the mahouts, had used his trunk to grab the royal ankle. He lifted His Lordship high in the air, and slammed him on the ground. Then he kicked the prostrate noble, stepped on his royal back, and walked off. Luckily, the rainy season had left the ground soft, so Sir Giles was able to sink into the mud rather than be crushed by the tremendous pachyderm. Although he emerged only slightly wounded, the event still served as an unsettling allegory for the French revolution, where the nobles were driven into the earth by the weight of the masses.

We took the field with the best of intentions, but it didn't take me long to realize how dangerous this game was. The ball rolled near my elephant's feet, and I tied to take a big swing as polo players did in movies.

But the mallet went every direction, missing the ball. The elephant continued running, and I watched the ball disappear behind us. Signaling the mahout, we backed up, and I took a second swing. This time, I held the mallet only inches from the ball and tapped it. The ball rolled a few centimeters, and I was very pleased with myself. Already having given up on swinging, like a man, I decided to content myself with dribbling. This was a girly technique, which involved just sort of dragging the ball along with your mallet as the elephant walked very slowly.

I was preoccupied with my granny maneuver, when a huge elephant from another team slammed into mine, bumping us for position. I only barely managed to pull my leg out I time, or it would have been crushed.

"Watch it!" I yelled at the player, who could probably buy me several times over.

Disregarding my warning, and my safety, he sung his two-and-a-half meter long mallet in a huge arch over his head, and drove the ball clean to the other end of the field. The problem was that when the stick came around, it nearly brained me.

"I'm through practicing," I told my Mahout.

I didn't like riding. And I was no good at swinging. Basically, I was as useless at elephant polo as I had anticipated being. Most people who read my articles and books of ultra macho physical adventures in the jungles and boxing rings of Asia would just assume that I was a good athlete. The truth is that I am the worst athlete who ever lived. I am strong, and have tremendous endurance, and an ability to focus and ignore pain. All of which serve me well in desert crossings and mountain expeditions. But apart from boxing, I cannot play any sports at all. When a group of people are choosing teams for softball or soccer, they always fight over who gets me. But I always tell them, I never played sports, apart from boxing and kung fu, as a kid. So I never developed any hand eye coordination. Also, I was deathly afraid of balls.

I would get in a boxing ring and fight a man who outweighed me by twenty kilos, but I would duck my head and cry like a baby if someone tossed a softball at me. I've even been known to run away from a Nerf ball.

As we approached the mounting house, the assistant asked me, "Stopping already?"

"Yes, I hate this game," I answered.

Christopher didn't do much better than I did. But as usual, he wasn't as negative as I was.

"It will still be loads of fun," he said.

Einarr, of course, not only took the sport seriously, but did fairly well at it. Pony polo experience had at least taught him how to swing a mallet and follow a ball. Which is what we ultimately decided one needed. Riding skills were useless, as the mahouts did all the work. It was necessary to speak Thai, and Christopher and I tutored Einarr in the basic rudiments of the language.

"If you speak Thai so well, why are you having so many misunderstandings with everyone?" asked Einarr.

"Because I just don't feel like speaking it right now," I answered. "They all make their living off of doing business with foreigners. They should learn to speak English."

"If you feel that way, you should leave their country."

"If we did, we'd all go to Cambodia and do the same stuff that we do here. But the Thais would all be unemployed. They need us. We don't need them."

"Well I like it here," said Einarr.

"I do too," I agreed. "I just don't always feel like speaking Thai."

"There's free whisky in the Chivas tent," said Christopher.

Once again, it was Christopher who found our commonalities. We all liked to drink. But I had to take it easy, because I had a big boxing match coming up in a few days.

That night we were invited to a players' dinner, as guests of the hotel. It was the first in a series of impossibly expensive meals that were scheduled for our entertainment. On the way in, I met the German team, sponsored by Mercedes, who were frightening in their knowledge of the game and their adherence to the rules. They approached me, and immediately began speaking German. Instinctively, I answered questions about elephant polo, and my Thailand experience. They even asked me about my movie and my book. Then it hit me.

"How did you guys know I spoke German?"

"We read the team profiles on the elephant polo website," explained Gerhard, the team leader. "Then we did a keyword search on your name, and found many articles about you."

"What was the name of the tribe you lived with in the jungle?" asked Berndt, one of the other team members.

"The Akha tribe," I answered. "Man, you guys really did your homework." It was actually a little scary how much of a person's life is available on the web, for any German who wants to know. "Have you guys played before?"

"Didn't you read the website?" asked Gerhard, amazed. "We were in the finals last year."

"Wow, so you have a huge advantage. And have you been here long, practicing?"

"No, only two weeks. But we practiced a lot on Germany. Our sponsors, Mercedes, gave us two cars to use. We specially ordered polo mallets from Thailand. Then we put saddles on top of the cars, and drove around, playing practice games. We also took intensive Thai lessons so we could talk to the mahouts."

We are going to lose so horribly, I thought.

The Tuskless Wonders, an all lady-boy team from Thailand, was definitely the media sensation. Photographers and reporters hovered around their table constantly. Other than giving interviews, they didn't mingle much with the other players, possibly because of the language barrier. But for as welcoming as everyone seemed toward the transgender team, there was a bit of us-and-them mentality going on. It was like the players wanted the lady-boys there as mascots, or to show how open they were. But then no one talked to them.

I like lady-boys as much as the next guy, that is assuming that the next guy is ambivalent about them. Truthfully, I never really understood the attraction. If you are into girls, then you could just date girls. And if you are into guys, you could date guys. So where did the lady-boy fetish fit into the whole greater scheme of dating? Whenever you ask people what they like about lady-boy shows in Bangkok, the answer is always, *They were so beautiful. And so real! You couldn't even tell they were guys.* So, once again, why not just go with real women? I have seen some real women who looked so much like women you wouldn't have thought for a minute that they were guys – and best of all, they weren't.

The one huge thing the lady-boys had in their favor, at least in my book, was that they were managed by a relentlessly self-promoting American named Yon. This guy knew how to get press. And his team was on almost every magazine or TV spot. (Pardon the pun. *TV*, in this instance, refers to television.) I would eventually wind up forming an alliance with Yon, but that story would come later.

The next afternoon I met the Kiwi Assassins, a team of ex-rugby players from New Zealand, who had struck it rich in real estate speculation. They were the one team that had less manners than me. But they still had more money. There was no justice in the world.

Where the other players seemed like the attendants of a fancy lawn party, The Kiwi Assassins were more like lads out for a good time. After the refined, posh English accents of the other players, it was refreshing to hear food referred to food as "tucker," alcohol as "grog," and lady-boys as "girl-guys." They showed up extremely drunk, unshaven, a day late, and missing a man. "We just don't know what happened to him," said Bruce, their team captain. "We were drinking Chivas in Bangkok. He was with us then. But later, we may have changed bars or gone to another city, still not sure about that one. Then we were in a limo, and there was more free Chivas...then it was night. And we were here, but Daren wasn't."

Even missing a man, the team still took up most of the room. All of their members were huge, mountainous men. On the website, (yes, I started doing research) it said that in addition to having been very famous rugby players, three of the members had been professional boxers, and one had been a national judo champion. It was a given that all of them were veterans of many a bar brawl.

The New Zealanders became dejected, when they realized that they were *not* allowed to hit the other players. "Why'd we even bothering coming then?" asked one of the team members.

At the Tuesday night social cocktail hour, Bruce

Manson, the leader of the team, had me in a corner, where, after draining most of the hotel's supply of liquor down his throat, he regaled me with tales of how he had personally maimed men with his bare hands, and how he had consequently come to be known as *Bruiser Bruce.*

"And after the rusty tuna can broke off, the hole was just big enough for me to slip my hand into his belly. And I was thinking to myself. You hear so much about the liver, but you never get to see one," Bruce was saying.

I was ready to vomit, or jump out the fire exit or both.

"*Do you?*" he yelled.

I had thought it was a rhetorical question. "No, you never get to see one," I agreed.

"That's right. And you certainly never get to feel one, to hold it in your hands, and know if your opponent had been a good man."

"True again."

Bruce kept advancing, getting more and more animated in his hand motions as he talked. I had been retreating the whole time. Now, there was nowhere to go. I had my back to the wall and was wedged into a corner by a very expensive armoire, which contained a display of pre-Lanna artifacts, none of which looked like it would be a formidable weapon with which to defend myself if Bruce lost his mind. On the other hand, maybe this was a blessing, because at least Bruce wouldn't be killing me with any of the expensive antiques.

"So, I reached in and..."

"Who's talking about their liver?" asked a very drunk woman in her fifties who had crashed the party. "I can drink any of you under the table, and my liver is fine. Solid, like the rock of Gibraltar."

"I believe that condition is known as *cirrhosis*." On second inspection of her aged features, I thought maybe the condition was called *rigamortis*.

"You think you could drink me under the table?" Began Bruce, forgetting me and the liver in the process.

"Of course I can. I have been a journalist for fifty-seven years. I've drunk with the best of them," continued the woman whose name was Paula.

While the two became drinking buddies, I dropped to my belly and crawled like a marine, emerging on the other side of the armor, which seemed like a fantasy world, where the party was still in progress and no one was threatening to cut out my organs.

This particular party was a press gig, so everyone in the room was either a member of the press or a player. In my case, I was both, which got more than a little confusing.

Players asked me who I was, and I said that I was with the press. I said this because I would need to interview them at some point, and it would seem strange, a player interviewing another player.

"Then where'd you get the jersey?" they'd ask.

"I am also on the Kuoni team. But I am covering the event for several travel magazines."

This never seemed to sit right with them. They regarded me as a gate crasher. But I knew the only real gate crasher was Paula. She was neither a member of the press nor a player. I was both.

"So, what is your connection to Kuoni Corp?" would be the next question.

"None," I'd answer truthfully.

"And what does Kuoni do?"

"I don't know?"

"Is it that you are a journalist, but the rest of the team work for Kuoni?"

188■

"No, we are all journalists, and none of us have the slightest idea who Kuoni is."

Then with that British reserve they would always give some non-committal answer, such as, "I see," or "Quite," or – best of all – "How fortunate for you." I never understood that last one. It seemed a little insulting, as if I couldn't pay for this vacation on my own. Well, I couldn't. But I didn't want other people pointing that out for me.

The members of the press were also confused, and while I made many friends among the press corps later, that first night was a bit frosty. "You are on team Kuoni, then, are you?" asked Vanessa, the reporter from *Leisure Travel UK*.

"Yes."

"And do you work for Kuoni?"

"No, I am a journalist."

Suddenly there was a bristle in her educated demeanor. It was as if she saw me as a potential threat.

"And you are on vacation?" she asked, leading the witness.

"No, I am on assignment. I am covering this tournament for a bunch of mags."

All the members of the press were the same. They were all a little standoffish until I assured them that the magazines that I wrote for were smaller than the ones they wrote for.

"Not only have you never heard of the magazines I write for, but neither has anyone else."

At this point I went from being a threat to being a kind of cuddly bear of a down-and-out journalist.

"And they all allow you to write the same story? I could never get away with that," she said, in amazement.

"They have no choice. The most any of them pays me is like fifty bucks. So, I have to sell the story ten times just to cover the cost of film and processing."

Vanessa seemed a little bit more at ease at this point. But I could also tell by the way she was scanning the crowd, that she felt it would be a waste of time talking to me, when she could be interviewing other players (real players sucking up to press people with good connections). With a muttered half excuse, she wandered back into the crowd. Once again, I was glad that the event lasted a full week, because everyone loosened up as time went on, and Vanessa and I became good friends. She did some research on me, online, and came back to ask me about my book which told the story of my solo crossing of the Taklamakan Desert. She was on her way to the Sahara and would also liked to have gone to China's great desert.

I think all the journalists, myself included, were under a lot of financial and time pressure, were used to having only a narrow window to get all the information they could, file their stories so they could get paid, and move on. But given the length of this story, we were able to slow down, smell the roses, and make friends.

While a week's long adventure was normal for me, some of my adventures ran months. Most journalists weren't used to being on a single assignment for this long. As the week went on, and they were more comfortable, they gave me some good advice.

On the financial side, they were fairly open about what they were making. Where I thought I was so poor, with my earnings for ten stories totaling about US$500, I found out I wasn't that far from the average wage. Most of them told me they were getting about five hundred Pounds, or about US$700 for the story. The difference, of course, was that they only had to deal with one magazine. But I still wasn't convinced if getting into one big magazine, once, was really getting them more exposure than what I was doing, which was as many as ten or even fifteen magazines per month. One cool advantage I had as the week went on was that I was the only journalist who was writing for local media and could get local support and help. It was an interesting trade off.

I wrote for small magazines, but they were known to the owners of the hotel and to local businesses, who gave me some support and free stuff while we were in town. And, of course, Christopher and I were the only members of the press core who spoke Thai.

The journalists from New York were the best paid of us all. Phil, who wrote for an international gay magazine, and Ming, who wrote for one of the largest web-based news portals, were both getting about US$4,000 for their story. Even better, once this event was over, they were being shipped to another of the Bekhenshire hotels to cover a food and wine show, for about the same amount of money.

The other teams were all easily recognizable and easily definable. There was a team from American Express, which contained professional horse polo champions from India and Sri Lanka. It was also clear why the members had been chosen. The British army team, for example, contained players from the British army horse polo team. But our team, Team Kuoni, remained an enigma.

Team Kuoni was sponsored by a faceless corporation, located somewhere, who none of us were familiar with or had any connection with. In fact, during the course of the week, we never met or heard from the corporation who paid the thousands of dollars for our participation. The three members of our team were myself, a budding adventure writer and kung fu film star from Brooklyn, Christopher, an itinerant poet and beverage connoisseur from England, and Einarr, a young Viking from the semi-autonomous Danish possession of the Faro Islands. The captain of our team was Robert Stockton, one of the richest men in Thailand, who at the age of twenty, had earned his first million dollars.

I had to agree with everyone else who asked, "What the hell are you people doing here?"

Rachel, the PR director and sort of coordinator for the entire event, was asking me just this question, when we heard Paula screeching, "I was taking photos before you had hair on your boils!"

"I've checked this woman out, but no one seems to know who she is," said Rachel, forgetting my Kuoni connection. "I asked her for her invitation, knowing full well that she didn't have one, but then she said that she was a journalist. But when I asked who she was writing for, she was very evasive."

I felt a bit guilty. The tickets to these events ran about eighty dollars, and if Paula was freeloading, I felt at least partly responsible.

"I sort of know who she is," I said, like a schoolboy coming clean.

"You? But what's your connection to her?"

"Paula, who I swear I had never met till yesterday, read one of my articles on the Internet about six months ago. She e-mailed the magazine and asked to be put in contact with me because she wanted my permission to reprint part of my writing. I had no objections, and we have been in e-mail contact ever since."

"So, you invited her?" asked Rachel, not just a little pissed off.

"Not exactly," I stuttered. "She wanted access to the players and the polo grounds. So, I promised her that I would help her get into any players' areas and anywhere that the press might not get to go, so that she could do a story. But I never said that she could gate crash at the dinners and parties, especially since that has nothing to do with doing a story."

"She said that she was doing a story on you? Is that true?"

"Yes, that was part of our deal. There were two conditions. First, we needed a photographer, and Christopher and I couldn't afford one. As Paula said that she had a photographer with her, we asked if in return for our help, we could use her photos. Next, since I was helping her gain access to the players, I asked that she also include me in her article. I'm sorry if this has caused you a problem."

"No, I guess it is OK. The Kiwi Assassins seem to like her. But she shouldn't be coming to any of the dinners."

The truth about Paula struck me as a very lonely woman from Canada who came to Thailand with the idea of writing a book. I wasn't sure if she had ever written a book before. But it was clear that she was very much alone in this foreign country, which was hot, and strange, and where everyone spoke a language she found it impossible to learn. My theory was that she just wanted a place to hang out and people to talk to. And pretending to be a journalist made her feel useful. Already two days into the tournament, we hadn't seen this photographer of hers. The only photos she had taken were with her digital camera, which was no better than my own Nikon or even Christopher's pocket digital.

Rachel was amazing at her job. It was unfathomable how many moving parts a large-scale event like this must have, but Rachel kept them all well oiled and in working order. During the entire week, there was not a single glitch. Even more amazing, when the event was over, most of us would go home. But Rachel would just move to Bangkok and manage another weeklong event with the food and wine show.

Through it all, not only did Rachel manage to be good humored and personal, but she also never stopped promoting her boss, Robert Stockton. His back-story, how he had become self-made millionaire, was fascinating. It was easy to see where someone would want to work for a man like him.

According to Rachel, Robert was an American by birth, but had been raised in Bangkok. While he was still in high school, he sold newspaper advertising at night. This came about because he had been a go-kart enthusiast and had asked the newspaper if he could write a go-kart column every week. The newspaper had said, *Yes*, but only under the condition that Robert sold enough ad space to cover the cost of the extra page of text. So, Robert went out and signed up all the go-kart-related businesses for ad space on his new page.

"His mom used to drive him and had to wait in the car while he held sales meetings," laughed Rachel.

By age seventeen he became the manager of the advertising department of Thailand's largest English language newspaper. But customers were told they could only buy ad space after 3:30 PM, when young Robert came into the office from his high school.

When he finished high school, Robert considered college, but decided that it would take time away from his business. So he dropped out and made his life long commitment to pursue the path of wealth. He took the twelve hundred dollars he had saved from selling ad space and used US$500 to file incorporation papers for each of two companies. One was an advertising company. And one was an office cleaning company. Robert had figured out that instead of selling ad space in one newspaper, he could sell packages, which included ads in all of them. And as for office cleaning, just one speculation, he decided that there were unlimited offices in Bangkok, and that they would all need to be cleaned. His remaining money, about US$200, he used to buy mops and cleaning supplies.

The gamble paid off. By the time he was twenty years old, Robert was a US dollar millionaire. He spent the rest of the last thirty-odd years pursuing risky businesses – the new things – and winning, time and time again. Today, among his possession are the Pizza Mansion, Thailand's largest chain restaurant, and a number of luxury hotels, including the Bekhenshire.

We were sitting in the Kuoni courtesy tent, waiting for our fist game to start, when a smiling, good-looking American, in his late forties, walked in and shook our hands. "I'm Robert," he said. "Who here is from Kuoni?"

For Christopher, Einarr, and me, this was the last straw. We had just assumed that Robert Stockton would have some connection to Kuoni. But we were wrong. And like us, it turned out that he had never heard of the corporation, neither did he know what they did. His next question seemed to be the last straw for him.

"If you guys don't work for Kuoni, then I can only assume that you were chosen for this team because you had polo experience. So, who's played before?"

Again, our answer disappointed him.

"We're journalists," I said, meekly.

The impression I got from Robert was that he had come mainly to find out who Kuoni was. But since that was impossible, he decided to leave and finish his business elsewhere.

"Of course, since I own this tournament, maybe I should play one chukka," he said. And that is just what he did. He played the first chukka. I substituted for him in the second, and we didn't see him again until the final day of the tournament.

One of the organizers came up to me, while Robert was playing the first chukka, and said, "Robert has to fly out right after this. So we have a car waiting."

"What time is his flight?" I asked.

The organizer laughed as if I were a naïve child. "It doesn't matter what time he goes. He owns the plane."

Of course he does. What was I thinking?

When it came my turn to play, I wasn't as excited as I could have been. I knew that I would suck at this game, as I did at all games. Our team hadn't scored a single point in the first chukka, and we were already losing, four to two. The only reason for the two was that we had a two-point handicap.

Elephant polo is basically horse polo, but played on an elephant. The game is played on a standard football pitch, with only three players on a side. No more than two players from each team may be at a single end of the field at a given moment, and no more than two elephants total may be in the *dee*, the area just in front of the goal. Other than that, it is all about hitting the ball, running, and passing – but very, very slowly. In elephant polo you often find yourself hanging off the side of the beast, trying to hit the ball. You look up and see two other elephants bearing down on you, and you suddenly forget the ball, and go for safety. When elephants collide, you would be best advised to kick your foot out of the stirrup and throw it up on top, where it can't get crushed. Yes, there is an element of danger.

But that is why elephant polo is my life.

I was rehearsing that line, "elephant polo is my life," hoping to use it in the post-game TV interview, when I noticed that we were losing, nine to zero. Apparently, while I had dozed off, dreaming of a bizzaro world where my team, Kuoni, composed entirely of journalists, were actually the winners, rather than the comic relief in elephant polo, the other team had scored again

I was wide open. My teammate, Christopher Laurence, reporter for *Chiang Mai City Beat*, passed the ball my way. With the quick reflexes of a man who doesn't want the game to end in a seven-zero defeat, I squeezed my knees into the animal's sides and jerked at the reigns. But nothing happened. For the hundredth time that day, I am reminded that I am riding an elephant, not a horse. And that single fact, along with the larger stick and the greater wealth of the players, was what separated elephant polo from horse polo.

In elephant polo you shout commands to your mahout, who, in theory, will steer the mighty pachyderm in the direction that you want. "Quick! Go Left!" I yell as I see the ball slowly rolling out of my reach. Again, nothing happened. Most mahouts don't speak English. I recalled, "*Bei kwa!*" I yell in frantic Thai. Obedient to the last, the mahout urges the animal to slowly turn right. "I mean *bei sei*," I corrected. By this time, our opponents, a bunch of filthy rich guys from private schools in England with accents like Mr. Howell from Gilligan's Island, have control of the ball again. The score jumps to eight-zero.

"Well," I thought in conciliation, "at least we won't loose seven-zero."

My feeling was that, going into the game already ahead by two, we should just have stopped there. I

Everyone else could afford to play polo. but my team was like the journalist charity team playing on scholarship.

Elephant polo was hard and dangerous. The elephants were big and I wasn't going to try and stoip them.

We lost every match. but we thought it wold be rude to win since someone else was paying

The Mahuts are an ancient race with their own distinct language and culkture. They have cared for Thailand's elephants for centuries.

I boxed for elephant awareness. But after the fight, I wasn't aware of much. In the end, I lost the fight. But it was one of the best fights of my life. No complaints!

The L A D Y B O Y S

mean, why go and ruin a perfect lead by actually playing? But the others were against this strategy. Now that we were losing, I expected an apology – but never got one.

The second half was boring for me and humiliating for all of us. I played the backfield where the ball never seemed to come. A chukka is only seven minutes. But it seemed to last an eternity, as I sat there in the heat with every eye in the world watching my lack of performance. And of course, once you start concentrating on your lack of performance, it prevents you from performing.

At the other end of the field, Christopher was involved in heavy scrimmage the entire time, and although the opposition continued to score goals, Christopher proved himself to be a valuable player. Einarr also won acclaim with several long drives of the ball and skillful elephant riding. He would become the team favorite and play in every chukka of the tournament.

The final score was eight to two – and would not be our worst defeat of the tournament. And to save the reader any unnecessary expectations, no, *we didn't score a single goal in the entire week of play.*

Once you got over the initial surprise of seeing people riding elephants on a soccer field, elephant polo became a bit boring. The elephants were just too slow, compared to horses. And play would often come to a complete stop when the ball became hidden under an elephant, or when one of the tremendous animals stepped on the ball, driving it into the ground. As I had work to do, I decided that I would write during the day, and only attend those games that I was playing in. The one exception was the most covered game of the tournament, the Kiwi Assassins v. the Tuskless Wonders.

If Lady Boys were one end of the spectrum of *quien es mas macho,* then the Kiwi Assassins were the other end. And there were no two teams which had a better built in rivalry and mass appeal than these two. There was a game between British army and Germany, but I was banned from the commentator's booth for that one, because it was felt that most of my comments were inappropriate.

Before the big match up, the Kiwi Assassins got very drunk. Actually, I think they were drunk anyway, the match was a coincidence. Bruce came to me, dejected, sweating, and a bit green around the gills.

"There's no way we can win," he whined. "We don't know how to play polo. And we are going against these girl guys. If we win, what did we do? Beat up a bunch of girls. That's nothing. And if we lose, we lose big." Bruce shook his head. "If we were allowed to hit them, I bet we could win."

I was picturing Bruce, with his eighteen-inch forearms, smashing one of the lady boys in the bridge of the nose. The sound of shattered bone was sickening. "I could grab her like this, and hit her like that!" he yelled, happy for a moment, flailing about with his knees and elbows. But then the reality set in again, and he wilted like a week-old rose. "But how can you hit someone on an elephant? Our only chance to win is to make a deal."

This sounded interesting. I have often been mesmerized by the pseudo-intellectual musings of Neanderthals.

"We're going to make a deal! We'll let the girl guys win the first game. And in return, they have to take me and my mates out on the town in Bangkok." Bruce smiled; he was picturing his big night on the town with the lady boys. "We'd rent a limo, and they'd take us around all night, showing us their town."

Town? Bangkok is bigger than New Zealand.

"But we wouldn't sleep with them!" he blurted.

I hadn't asked.

"Maybe we would," he immediately amended. Then he went through his team roster. "He would. He might if he had enough grog in him. He wouldn't. That one, if he had enough grog, probably couldn't. I probably would..."

By the time the match started, everyone had heard of Bruce's plan. Oddly, no one had heard if the plan had been accepted by the lady-boys. Rachel's theory was that the lady-boys hadn't even been consulted.

"This way," she said, "if the Kiwi Assassins lose, they can say that it was because of the deal. And if they win, it was because the deal was rejected."

Before the game the Kiwi Assassins lined up in formation, in the center of the field, across from their rivals, and did the *Haka*, the Maori (New Zealand) native war dance. That moment was the single most photographed event of the tournament, and Rachel's value to the Robert Stockton Empire shot through the roof when the All Black's Haka made it into the New York Times. That was the biggest press exposure elephant polo had ever received.

The Haka ended with the Kiwi Assassins extending their tongues to the lady-boys – perhaps this was a pre-cursor of what would happen in the back of the limo in Bangkok.

Yon was such a good promoter that he had prepared his girls for this moment. Unrattled by tongue sticking, the lady-boys countered with a dance of their own, a brief cheerleading routine, which accentuated their flawless feminine bodies.

"Are they real?" was a constant murmur, which followed them throughout the weeklong event.

The routine ended with the lady-boys extending their exquisitely shaped bottoms. It was the perfect conclusion to the war like dance of the Kiwi Assassins. Afterwards, the New Zealanders, in an act of classic chivalry, presented flowers to the girls and picked them up, posing for photographers.

Basically, between the elephants, the lady-boys, the Haka, and the cheerleading, elephant polo had become a show with everything – except Yul Brenner.

After the build up, the game itself was just icing on the cake. But having the ladyboy team at the tournament really spiced things up. And they spawned a new greeting: *Still got your trunk?* I wondered how far the game had come from its ultra macho beginnings in the British Colonial Expeditionary Force in India.

The teams mounted up. Sam Nang, the most attractive of the lady-boys, rocked gently back and forth, applying rouge to her cheeks as her ten ton elephant ambled onto the playing field.

"Good luck," an assistant shouts, handing her the three-meter-long polo mallet.

"How's my make up?" she answers back.

A girl must know her priorities, and with photographers packed in like sardines, looks mattered more than substance. Flashbulbs popped like the opening night of the Grammies, and the official gong sounded, signaling that the elephant polo had begun.

Big, powerful, muscular, immovable, majestic, and dung. All adjectives used to describe the immense beasts, which bear the players up and down the field.

Charming, dainty, gorgeous, pristine, beautiful, and maybe/maybe not. All adjectives used to describe the members of the Tuskless Wonders.

In a field of massive gray pachyderms, it was refreshing to see the tiny splashes of pink from their

=205

uniforms. Although they always kept their girlish demeanor and lady-like behavior, the team was no pushover when it became heated play. Perhaps straddling a large sweaty beast may seem like an ordinary Tuesday night to most of us, but the Tuskless Wonders did it with style.

In the pre-game hype, the two teams had displayed chivalry and ladylike demeanor, respectively. But once play began, no quarter was given. New Zealand scored an early goal against the Tuskless Wonders. With Powder-Puff resolve, they rallied, stole the ball from the Kiwi Assassins, and drove it home, tying the score. The girls had several near misses, almost scoring a goal, but either fouling or going just short. In the end, the Kiwis won by a single goal.

They had lost the match. But for the Tuskless Wonders, just playing in the tournament was a huge victory.

I felt that the Tuskless Wonders should be applauded for their in-your-face, yes-I-am-different behavior. And kudos went to the Thai society, and the event sponsors, who were ready to just let girls be girls. But as with all ladyboy affairs, the question came to mind, does Thailand tolerate gay men? Or, does Thailand tolerate gay men who dress as women? If they wanted to test the limits of gay tolerance in Thailand, perhaps next year they should form an all-gay team, called The Beefcake Go-Go Boys. The team uniform could be silver boots and a gold sequined thong. Perhaps the official team greeting could be *Is that your trunk or are you just happy to see me?*

The Kiwi Assassins did disappear to Bangkok that night, but they claimed that they were going to a sponsor's dinner. Of course, we will never know what really happened.

At breakfast the next morning Christopher and I got on my favorite discussion topic. I really enjoyed talking about how poor I was.

"Did you know Phil is getting US$5,000 for this story?" I asked.

"Yes," said Christopher.

"I am selling it ten times. But I have one magazine who is only planning to pay me US$20 and another will give me US$40."

"I don't even get that," said Christopher. "I am on salary at *City Beat*, so all I get is my weekly salary, which is only about US$175. Einarr's scholarship from the Danish government is twice that, and he is an intern."

"The big guys also get everything paid for. Do you get your expenses covered?" I asked.

"Not all of them."

I laughed. "Small time journalism is the funniest, coolest job in the world. We get to go places and do stuff that most people can only dream of. But we have taken a vow of poverty."

At first, Christopher and Einarr were laughing along with me. But then Christopher got serious, almost angry.

"Why don't you talk a little louder?" he said. "Everyone can hear you in this dinning hall. If you keep telling people how poor you are, you will always be a small time journalist. Maybe you are sitting next to someone who was going to offer you a better job."

Christopher had a point. I guess I had relaxed too much and was letting players and hotel staff hear conversations that should have been reserved for other journalists. Once again, it illustrated the difficulty in playing the dual role of player and journalist. On the other hand, I thought it was the funniest topic of discussion, and couldn't get off of it.

"Do you know that Phil gets, like, US$4 per word? So, if he writes that I went to the bathroom yesterday, he already makes more money than I will get for this story."

"You see what Christopher means, Antonio! That is just the attitude that is holding us back," said Einarr.

Who asked you, Dutch Boy? Get back on my paint can where you belong.

"And even worse, his pay is probably like *Scrabble*. Bathroom is a compound word. So he probably gets a double word score. If he uses it on a Wednesday, he gets triple word payout."

"Could you please stop? You think you're funny. But you turn people off," insisted Christopher. "Like yesterday, when someone asked you who was the fourth member of our team you said, 'It's some rich guy whose name I forgot.'"

"I couldn't remember his name. Is that a crime?" I explained, in my own defense.

"It *is* when he's paying your way. Besides, his PR director was standing right behind you when you said it."

Christopher had a point. I knew I was callous. But it was unstoppable.

"Christopher's right!" admonished Einarr. "You keep making a big deal about how expensive everything is, and that it is free. But you have to learn to play it cool, like me, and just expect everything to be rich and free."

"Not being from a socialist country, I am not used to everything being free," I pointed out.

Normally our breakfast was a lavish buffet, which ran for hours. On this day, a chef, all dressed in whites, came around, asking if we preferred omelets or crepes.

"Is that complimentary?" asked Einarr.

"Of course," answered the chef.

"In that case, I'll have five of each," he said. Einarr liked to eat as much as Christopher liked to drink.

After the waiter had gone, Christopher looked at Einarr in surprise. "Five?"

"They were free! Could you believe that?"

"I could," I said. "In fact, I expected it."

Christopher laughed. I was taking Einarr's advice, but he wasn't pleased.

"In fact, the reason I was late this morning was that I expected a free breakfast in bed, as I am accustomed to."

"You're an asshole," laughed Christopher.

"I'm quite tired now. Normally, I don't have to chew my food myself. I have people who do it for me. I expect it. But this place is a dump."

Phil, the journalist from the big gay magazine in New York, came over and joined us. "Do you guys know where I could get one of those jerseys? They are fabulous?"

"You just have to expect them," I answered.

"What?"

"He means only team members get them," explained Christopher.

"How did you guys get on a team and I didn't?" he asked. Phil really did expect everything, and in the end, he always got it. I learned to respect Phil as the week went on. But the question still came to my mind, *Why did I respect Phil, but not Einarr.* Probably because Phil's insistence that he be given everything was not only successful but also very genuine, whereas Einarr's insistence that I pretend to expect everything was a pre-programmed parrot response of a limousine liberal, from a country of limousine liberals, who could afford to have opinions which were contrary to reality. That was one reason I respect Phil. The others were that he was actually a journalist, not a poser, and that he made more money than me.

"I flew all the way here from New York. The least they could do is put me on a team," complained Phil.

"Now that Robert Stockton has left, there is an opening on our team," suggested Christopher.

"And you could borrow my extra jersey," said Einarr.

As much as I hated to admit it, Einarr had been right. Actually, Christopher had been right. Einarr had only been a parrot. One of the reasons Phil was so much more successful than us could definitely have been because of his attitude, which demanded special treatment. The primary difference between us was that, while Phil appreciated the free accommodations, he could have paid for the room if he needed to. He also didn't fill his backpack with food from the free press buffets or steal soap from the bathroom.

The deal was made. We were now complete, a team of four journalists, none of whom knew anything about polo. A more perfect, and yet pathetic team, could never have been formed.

Breakfast was always a good opportunity to talk to the other journalists and find out what mistakes I was making in my career. Jeff was one of my role models among our group. He was a photographer who worked for an image library based out of Singapore. They flew him all around the world, shooting photos, which would be stored in their archives. When a magazine needed a photo of a bunch of monks, or of a boxing match, or of George W. Bush, they could just log onto the library, select the photos they wanted, and pay a royalty. Jeff worked for one of the most respected libraries in the world, and he made a lot of money. He was also one of the only other Americans – other than myself, Phil, and the girl from the web-portal magazine.

Jeff had been around a lot and had seen more than most people. Best of all, he really enjoyed swapping funny stories. When we got on the subject of the deserts in China, I told him that I discovered some semi-nomadic tribal people living a thousand kilometers from nowhere, who ate bagels as a supplement to their diet.

"Since I can't imagine that tons of New Yorkers have been to that particular part of the desert, to introduce them to our favorite breakfast food, then I would have to believe that these people have been eating bagels for centuries," I said.

"And that region belongs to China now?" he asked.

"Yes, they grabbed it right after they grabbed Tibet."

"Oh great!" shouted Jeff. "China always makes these outrageous claims. Like, for example, China has the oldest minted coins. So, they claim to have invented money. The Peking Opera is older than Greek theater. So, they claim to have invented entertainment. Now they will claim they invented breakfast."

I tended to fit in better with the journalists than with the players. But there was one player, however, who I found I had a lot in common with. Will Hedin had quit his phenomenally lucrative office job, in order to pursue an exciting career as a bush pilot. He had flown into and out of some of the craziest and scariest places in Southeast Asia and made a national geographic documentary about his work. He took freelance assignments, training drug interdiction pilots in

Thailand, teaching them to land planes on short runways in the jungle while they were being shot at. As is the way of successful people, even after having left his big money job to pursue his dream, his dream became his next big money job. In Bangkok, he had been given the staring role in an aviation feature film, due to be released shortly. When I went on-line and saw his personal website, I felt so jealous. Not only had he chronicled his amazing adventures, but there, in the online shop, was the much-coveted yellow-rimmed box which contained his National Geographic documentary. National Geographic had been my dream since I was a child. And Will Hedin was already there.

Will was just one more of those chance meetings, which leaves an indelible mark on you and motivates you to succeed.

We were playing a game in the early afternoon, so we headed out to the polo grounds, to allow Christopher and Einarr enough time to soak up sufficient quantities of free Chivas. Christopher enjoyed the liquid refreshment, which loosened his tongue and powered his British whit and phenomenal word usage. He would often wax into poetic recitations or Ph.d-level plays on words. But he would then change gears, one hundred eighty degrees, and take the piss of my Brooklyn accent, using phrases such as *Hey, how you doin'?* Or *What am I? Some kind of mook or something?*

Einarr also enjoyed the endless gallons of free Chivas, but being basically Danish, he was disappointed by the free buffet. "How can you have a seafood buffet that doesn't include mammals?" he would ask, searching for chunks of his beloved wale blubber.

212∎

Our first all-journalist team match-up was the best. Christopher had already proven himself a good defender. Einarr was good on attack, and Phil made sure that our hair looked good. "There is no sin in playing poorly, only in looking poorly," he told us.

Having given up on ever winning a game, our new goal was simply to preserve our dignity. We marched into combat, chanting our mantra *Tie game! Tie game!*

It was a heated battle, with the ball being passed back and forth, with some wonderful action and teamwork. Phil saved me several times, and I did the same for him. We began to refer to our end of the field as the New York defense. We still lost, without scoring even a single point. But, managed to defend so well that the score was only 4 to 2, the smallest margin by which we would ever lose a game. We were high on how well we had done, but no one else understood the triumph of our personal victory. When they saw us celebrating in the air-conditioned Chivas tent, they would ask, "Why so happy? Did you win?"

"No. Our goal was a tie score."

"Did you get that at least?"

"No, but it was the closest we have ever come."

The next match-up was British Army v. Germany. Christopher was asked to be guest commentator, with the proviso that I not be allowed near the microphone. I had already distinguished myself as a colorful character who made off-color remarks as an occupation. It was feared that I would insult one or the other of the teams. Actually, it was feared that I would insult the Germans. Of course, when I showed up at the booth, with two drink trays full of Chivas, Christopher invited me in. Minutes later, the rain started, and Christopher began his narrative.

"It's a rainy day in Britain, as her majesty's finest prepare to do battle," he began. We really believed that the rain would favor the Brits. But all the practice the Germans had done was really paying off. Before we knew it, they were ahead by nine. It was as bad as many of our own defeats.

At the half, the British players all rode over to shake hands with the Germans.

"Ah, a mark of true British sportsmanship," said Christopher. "And the Brits, in their finest tradition of decorum, are unflappable in the face of such overwhelming odds."

"The Brits are used to withstanding German onslaughts," I added. Christopher pulled the microphone away from me and continued his banter from the other side of the booth.

"The question in everyone's mind is just how long can the British hold out against such a pounding?"

"About five years," I said.

In the second half, Christopher had some fun with the commentary, treating elephant polo as if it were soccer. Every time the Germans scored, he yelled, "GOOOOOOaaala!" as they do in Latin America. Then, he decided that since soccer was a world game, played on cable stations in every country, he began switching channels. One minute he did his commentary in Spanish. The next was French. He had me do the German. His Spanish one was best. "*Que excitente! Los players hacen tacos y burritos en todo el game.*" The Cuban channel was stuck on a pro-Fidel rally. "*Que vive Fidel! Viva la raza! Vive Che Guevara! Vive la Cuba Libre!*"

The only down note to an excellent day of elephant polo was that he was in rare form, bringing the words *culture clash* to some new, never before imagined level. It started in the van on the way to the game, when I asked Bea, in both Thai and English, if we could stop at Seven-Eleven and get some coffee.

"You go Seven?" she asked, using the Thai name for the chain.

"Yes, I go seven," I repeated. Now I had told her three times.

"And you?" she asked Christopher.

"If the van goes there, then I will also have to go there, won't I?" he began. But then quickly changed to "Yes, I go to Seven."

"And you?" she asked the Dutch boy.

"OK."

I thought this was a weird line of questioning, but if it got me where I wanted to go, I didn't care.

Bea nodded, and we continued to drive. We drove past fifty Seven-Elevens. When we reached the polo grounds I asked, "Bea, why didn't we go to Seven?"

"Yes."

"No 'Yes'! Why didn't we go to Seven?" I was asking everything twice, in both languages.

Christopher also asked in Thai.

"Yes, there are many Seven," she said proudly.

"We only need one. And you need to take us there," I said.

I almost flipped out. But Christopher intervened and convinced Bea to turn the van around, drive back to town. Once there, he managed to get her to stop at the eighth Seven-Eleven that we came to. I would have given anything to know what she had understood, or why she had done this.

Later, while we were waiting to play, I sat my full cup of coffee down on the table and was about to drink from my water bottle, when the cap came off and water went all over me. I put the water bottle down, brushed the water of my body, and picked up my chair to shake the excess water off. While I was doing this, Bea ran over, grabbed my full coffee cup, and threw it in the trash.

"Why did you do that?" I asked, not comprehending.

"Sorry."

"Not sorry. Why did you do that?"

"Sorry."

The Dutch boy tried to intervene. "She doesn't speak English," he said.

"I know she doesn't speak English. But why did she throw away my coffee? Lot's of people don't speak English, but they don't throw away my coffee. My Uncle Enzio came over on the boat from Sicily. He lived in America thirty years, but he never learned to speak English. And yet, he never threw away my coffee."

"But you are looking at it from our perspective. Maybe in her culture it made sense to throw away your coffee."

"That is the stupidest excuse I have ever heard in my life," I said.

The coffee incident was trivial, in that it was just a cup of coffee. But it was significant in that it left me asking, *Why? Why? Why? Why?* And I wasn't getting answers. This was the beginning of the end for me and Bea.

As much as my relationship with Bea had been rocky, that night things got even worse. There was a big swanky wine dinner planned at another hotel. Rachel had assured us that we had tickets. We really wanted to go, but we wanted to make sure that Bea understood.

"Did you puck up our tickets?" we asked her the morning of the day before.

"Yes."

"Did you pick up our tickets?" we asked the afternoon of the day before.

"Yes."

"Did you pick up the tickets?" we asked the night before.

"Yes."

Twice more, the day of the event, we asked if she had picked up our tickets. And, always the answer was *Yes*.

When we got to the dinner, there was a huge discussion, in Thai, between Bea and the hotel staff. When it ended, Bea said, "Since we don't have tickets, would you mind just paying $50 each?"

Would we mind paying $50? She asked as if it were nothing. This was a huge sum of money for us.

"But I thought you had our tickets," I said.

"No, not have," she said simply. There was no apology or mention of why she didn't have our tickets. And when I asked why she had told us several times that she had the tickets, when she didn't actually have them, she blamed us.

"You said that Rachel give tickets for everything."

"Yes, we did say that Rachel arranged our tickets. But we told you to pick them up from Rachel." Not only had we told her, but this was the standard procedure. None of the players were expected to handle their own tickets.

She didn't counter. She just repeated, "Because not have tickets, must pay $50."

I could see that Christopher was disappointed. He really wanted to attend the dinner. Even worse, all of the other players saw us arguing with the staff, and eventually leaving the dinner. It was so embarrassing. I almost demanded that Bea pay the US$100 for us.

By the time we got back to the hotel, most of the food at the free press buffet had been eaten. And again we were humiliated at having to come back with our tails between our legs. Phil flipped out when he heard our story. "A wine dinner? Why wasn't I invited?"

He was livid. And actually, once again, you could easily say he kept asking for the moon and the sun. But his arguments made a lot of sense. He was a columnist for the largest food and wine magazine in the world. If you had a wine dinner, wouldn't he be at the top of the invitee list? I was a columnist for the largest martial arts magazine in the world. One could easily say that it was more important to invite Phil than me.

I think this was the character someone from New York, whether it be Phil or myself. Although almost anyone would agree with the logic of this line of reasoning, most people would just lay down and accept whatever life gave them. The New Yorker would demand what was his.

"Don't worry," I consoled Phil. "Even if you had been invited, your invitations would have been lost, and you'd have been turned away and humiliated like us."

The one good point was that I had managed to finally reach Jorge, the guy who ran the boxing tournament where I was to be fighting. If I had reached him earlier in the week, then I would have had time to make arrangements with the press. I had even brought my own fliers from Cambodia, which I had planned to have kids distribute during the fight.

With less than twenty-four hours notice, all I was able to do was to go around and tell each and every player and press member. It was weak. And it sounded like some weird form of brag. But it had to be done. There was no point in fighting in obscurity.

After he had heard me tell nearly fifty people about the fight, Einarr said to me, "Is that all you do is self-promote?"

"Mostly," I agreed.

"I have been living with you for nearly a week now, and I feel I don't know you."

"You know me. I am the guy who relentlessly self-promotes."

Outwardly, I laughed. But inwardly, I had been worrying for years. No matter what I did – whether it was professional sports, adventure travels, or writing, or investment banking – I did it with tremendous focus, and I excluded everything else from my life. If I wasn't working on something or working toward something, I had no idea what to do with myself, and no idea of what to talk about.

I had always assumed that other people were working towards some goal or series of goals as I did. But I was beginning to realize there were people who just worked at a salaried job, with no real plans of where they hoped to wind up. For entertainment they drank, watched TV, chatted on the Internet, or did whatever it was that they did. But the point was, there was no goal. They weren't working towards anything.

I talked to all of the richer journalists about the career, finding out how I should be marketing myself, and what I should be doing to make it. After I had gathered info, and my brain was full, I would go to Christopher and do a brain dump. Telling him everything helped me process information. At the same time, I hoped that I was helping him, since he wasn't asking as many of those kinds of questions.

Finally, Christopher put his hands up for me to stop. "I can't hear anymore. I know more about your career than I do my own," he said.

It hit me that the reason Christopher wasn't asking

was because he didn't want to know.

Not for the first time, I wondered just who I was and where I belonged. Cambodia wasn't my home. Thailand wasn't my home. These weren't my people. When I choose to, I could speak their language and live as they lived. When I chose to, I could criticize and demean them, separating myself into my own cult of exclusivity. Was this how other people lived?

I always believed I would be a huge success. And I believed it was this aspect of my personality that would get me there. But I also believed it was this aspect of my personality that would keep me lonely, and that would prevent me from enjoying or even recognizing success when it came.

Einarr was right. But on the other hand should I live like him? He was ten years younger than me but had a tremendous beer belly. It was well known that the only time he ever got sex was when he paid for it. He was making almost as much money as me, but this was a grant form his government. It wasn't something he had achieved on his own. He was nearly thirty and hadn't held a job yet. And he had no idea, and barely a care what he would do with the rest of his life.

"I hate being poor," I admitted "And I know that every article I write, and every article that is written about me, and every movie I act in, is one step closer to me getting bigger financial contracts for my writing, and one step closer to wealth and fame, which will allow me to live indoors, and eat on a regular basis, and not worry about money."

Once again, Einarr missed the point. "If you want to succeed as a writer, you can't do it by being *famous*. You do it by being *good*."

This statement illustrated the difference between us, and maybe the difference between me and everyone else who hasn't made it yet. A belief that it was talent, and not marketing, that brought you success was a naïve belief that would forever hold people back. Another one of the fundamental differences between me and most people was that I was willing to admit that I wanted to make it. And since I hadn't made it yet, this meant I was currently a failure. By never stating that they wanted to make it, people were fine with where they were at the moment.

That night there was a huge party on the beach, sponsored by none other than Chivas. The food, the music, the alcohol...everything...was incredible. I knew that of the thirty or so people and press who said that they would come watch my fight, very few, if any, were actually going to accompany me. I walked through the crowd, saying goodby, and was surprised at the number of people who agreed to come.

Christopher and Einarr were first on the list. I half expected them to say that this was my gig, and I should do it alone. Besides, they were leaving free alcohol. But they looked at me like I was nuts. "We are your team, how could we let you go alone?" As much as Einarr and I had our differences, I appreciated he and Christopher coming with me.

Next, the Germans, true to their nature, stood up from their half-eaten dinner and escorted me out to the van.

"But you didn't finish eating," I said.

"Yes, but we promised."

During the four years that I lived in Germany, we referred to this type of behavior as the *German conundrum*. It was easy to write Germans off as unfriendly and impossible to get to know. But at the same time, if a German makes you a promise, it is a promise for life.

Even more, they will only use the word *friend* to describe an incredibly close relationship, and maybe just twice or three times in a lifetime. But when they said *friend*, it had real meaning. A German would drive all night, in the snow, to pick up a friend whose car had broken down. I have seen them do it. The Germans always say of Americans, *They are all so polite, and smiling, and friendly. But when you need help, no one comes.* Not only did the entire German team members and their wives come, but they drove us there in their Mercedes land rover.

Paula made it to the fight, and she actually brought a professional photographer with her. It was the only time that we saw this guy, but I was so grateful. His photos were excellent.

Minutes before my fight started, Will Hedin and his teammate, Juan Rodriguez, a wealthy landowner from Argentina, showed up. That meant a lot to me. Will was an adventure guy like me. He embodied everything masculine there was. He read Hemingway. He was a stud with the women. He spoke perfect Thai and had the whole country jumping through hoops. And, of course, the press were constantly flocking around him. After me, I believe he was the single most written about player in the tournament.

When the New Zealanders had done their Haka war dance, Will's eyes glazed over, in a kind of combat ecstasy. "They are warriors man," he said, through his tears. "They are retired warriors, and they are beautiful."

Jorge had asked me if I wanted any money, apparently the going rate of a fight in Huahin was 5,000 baht, or a bit over US$100. If that were the case in Cambodia, I would use boxing to supplement my income.

As much as I needed the money, I refused it, asking him, instead, to give it to the elephant conservatory. In the end, the money never made it to the elephants, however. I didn't want to touch the money, so I asked Rachel to send someone from the hotel. But with the tournament, and the fact that this was my own personal event, not a scheduled event, my request fell through the cracks. After the fight, when I asked Christopher to write the press release, he was a genius. He never said that I raised money for the elephants. He said that I was fighting to raise awareness of the elephants. That way I couldn't be blamed for the money not arriving at the conservatory.

In Cambodia I had been training two-and-a-half hours per day, preparing for a big televised fight. But my coach was having trouble nailing down a contract with the networks. They kept pushing the date forward, and I had to try and maintain peak condition for that much longer. Finally, after a month of delays, I broke and started eating like a pig again. Then, I missed my final week of training before leaving for Thailand. Now I had been in Thailand for a week, without training. Basically, I wasn't fit anymore. So, I asked Jorge if I could do a two round exhibition with headgear.

Thinking that we were on our way to a free dinner, Paula had weaseled her way into our team van and for some reason, insisted on being present at this meeting.

"I'm a journalist. I haven't really been training," I told Jorge.

Paula jumped in with "Yes, you've been training. You train all the time…"

"Paula!" I yelled, cutting her off. I was so annoyed. I didn't need her speaking for me. And this was serious. If I got matched up with the wrong guy, I could get hurt.

Originally, Jorge said *Yes* to my terms. Later, however, he said, "I am sorry. We have to make it three rounds, and no headgear."

I agreed. Jorge wasn't trying to pull the old switcheroo. He was just being fair. I was walking in off the street. He had no idea who I was. Then I was asking him to put me on the card at the last moment. And I was dictating terms. The fans would be paying money for their tickets. It wouldn't be fair for them to have to sit through an exhibition. So I agreed to a real fight.

Jorge had asked me to fight last, after the regularly scheduled five fights. But as long as I was making selfish requests, I asked him to bump me up in the order, so that my friends could get back to the hotel. In the end, I went on third. Jorge had told me earlier in the day that his son weighed eighty-five kilograms, the same as me. And I was very worried that he would match me up with his son, so that he could look good. But it turned out that Jorge was a fair man, and he matched me with an eighty-five kilograms Thai guy, which was fine with me.

The regular Thai boxers are usually extremely lean and muscular. Even when they only weigh sixty-file kilograms, they are built like Schwarzeneger. My second hope was that I wouldn't look across the ring and see one of those perfectly muscled Thai bodies blown up to eighty-five kilograms. That would have been to intimidating, especially since I am usually nearly twenty years older than my opponents. But my opponent turned out to be a young Thai, about twenty-four years old, my weight, but much taller than me, with a big reach. The fact that he was barefoot, and that this was Thailand, lead me to believe that he was a professional muay thai (Thai kick boxing) fighter.

I was nervous, and I knew that the two weeks off would greatly reduce my cardio fitness. I wished that my coach, Patty, could have been there. But because of a crossed communication, I misunderstood that he was waiting by the phone for me to tell him when to come, as opposed to waiting by the phone to hear the results, as I had thought.

So, I had no corner men, save for two Thais who spoke no English, and Christopher, who was not only drunk but had a beer in one hand and a cigarette hanging from his lips. "You'll kill him," he told me, giving me a rub down with his free hand. The cigarette made me cough, but I was still grateful to have my friend there. It was the most perfect corner I could have hoped for.

When your cardio is down but you are a hard puncher, it is probably better to go for an early win by knock out – or at least this was my strategy, since I wasn't sure if I had the wind to go three rounds. The bell sounded for the first round, and I came out with a flurry of punches. Patty had stressed working off the jab. "Keep your hand in his face, and he can't hit you," he had said.

I was throwing mostly straight punches, in rapid succession, as I moved forward. The opponent backed up, and backed up, till I had him on the ropes, pounding away at him.

Believe it or not, one of the things you forget to do when you aren't training every day is that you forget to hit hard. That may sound strange, but it isn't that unusual if no one is in your corner, telling you what to do; you go through the motions, throwing easy punches. Had someone been there to remind me, I would have loaded up on those punches. And there is no way that anyone could have survived. I hit my opponent so many times in the first round that he should have been dead. When the bell rang, I had him on the ropes. I really thought I had a good chance of winning a clean sweep victory.

In the corner, Christopher was a little bit sloppy, spitting beer on me, while the two Thai guys rubbed me down. I always liked that rub down in the corner, and usually didn't want to return to the fray. It made my groin protection too tight.

"Your doing great," he said.

"Thanks. I just wish Mick was here," I said, quoting *Rocky Three*.

"There is no tomorrow, Rock," Answered Christopher.

Christopher and I played so well off of each other that I was wishing this wasn't a real fight, so that we could have more fun with it.

"We gave you water. You got two Thai boys rubbing you with lotion. What more do you want?" he asked.

"If Patty were here, he'd be giving me advice."

Christopher thought a minute. "Alright, just what would Patty be doing for you right now?"

"Just go out there and kill him," suggested Christopher.

When the second round started, he had obviously gotten some good advice in his corner, because he came out fighting. I was still winning the second round when the muay thai fighter did the only thing muay thai fighters know how to do.

Thai fighters classically have terrible hands, but their kicks are devastating. But when it comes to Western boxing they are like children. They hold their hands too low, and their elbows are too far apart, leaving their face and body wide open. They aren't taught to jab or to throw combinations. But the one thing they can do is throw a huge right hook, much too long of a hook for boxing. But it has power, and it lands on the temple. I knew this. I also knew that I had a tendency to drop my left hand when I was throwing combinations. But I got tired and careless, and no one was there to tell me differently. Suddenly, I felt that huge hook catch the side of my head.

The punch was hard and sent a rumble all the way through my body, down to my toes. Luckily, he didn't follow up with anything. So, I shook it off, and continued my barrage. He was backing up and backing up. I had him on one set of ropes, and now he spun out and I followed him, trapping him on the other set of ropes. It looked like we would just stay there till the end of the round, when he hit me with another of those hooks. It landed right on the same part of my head. The hook was big, and going so wide, that I couldn't see it out of the corner of my eye. "It is the punch that you don't see that hurts you," Patty had warned me.

Although I had slowed down in the second round, I was still dominating, till we got into a far corner, and he landed that same, huge right-hook to the side of my head. It hit me so hard that I almost went down. Everything went numb, and my opponent was very far away. So, I fell forward and grabbed hold of him. It only takes about eight seconds to recover from a near-knock out. I tied him up, and held on with all my might. Slowly, I felt myself coming round. I also felt the ref trying to separate us. So, I lifted the opponent at the hips, and rotated him into the corner, putting my body between the referee and the opponent. Now it would have taken a crow bar to separate us. Once again, I was reminded of so many nights in Chiang Mai.

By the time the ref managed to separate us, I had recovered so much that there was no need for a standing eight-count, and he just let the fight continue. I charged in, got him on the ropes, and the round ended with me pummeling him. I had done what fight journalists call *stealing a round*. This means losing a round until the last fifteen seconds, then having a huge rally, which leaves an imprint in the judges mind. They always remember best the last thing that they saw. Going into the third round, I was tired. The round was about even. But then he hit me with that same right, and I felt some of my strength leaving me. He hit me again. And each time, I got weaker. I still managed to get him on the ropes once or twice, but there was no fire left in me. Then, he hit me so hard that I lost my mouthpiece. The ref gave me a standing eight count. I was completely numb, as if I had had a stroke. But no fighter ever wants to quit. So, when the ref asked, I said I was fine. He didn't look convinced, but he let the fight go.

As soon as he gave us the signal I came out swinging. But I was swinging in a dream. It was like being drunk and high on ether. It was like that episode in Bugs Bunny, where the ether can drops on the floor, and the mad scientist chases Bugs Bunny. They are both running in slow motion, like in a dream, and the mad scientist is saying, "C-o-m-e b-a-c-k, h-e-r-e r-a-b-b-i-t."

Luckily, the bell rang, or I would have been knocked out.

The decision was quick and fair. I had lost. But it had been a good fight.

The journalists and foreign visitors were all smiling. One of my editors had come in with the referee from the elephant polo, and they gave me a hearty congratulations. Two other big editors were there. I had no idea that that so many people wanted to come and watch the boxing journalist. They both said that they had bumped my stories up in the queue and would be using them in the following month's issue. All told, that single boxing match probably brought me about a month's salary in terms of work previously submitted which would normally not have been accepted. The weeks following the tournament proved to be a huge turning point for me. I finally got a big break. But I didn't know that at the time. I just knew that I had had a great fight, and I respected my opponent. I thanked Jorge heartily for his help.

Back at the hotel, the Chivas party was winding down. If there had been food, I'd have eaten it. The free bar was closed, and I ordered a coke and a water from the regular bar, which cost me six dollars. I went straight to bed.

We had originally been scheduled to play the next morning at 9:00 AM. But the schedule was changed to 2:00 PM, which was good, because I was going to need a good night's sleep after such a hard fight. I was awoken, from a dead sleep, by the telephone.

"Toni, wake up and play polo." It was Bea.

I thought maybe I had slept till afternoon. It had happened before. Once, after losing a fight in New York, I slept nearly thirty-six straight hours.

"What time is it?" I mumbled through my haze.

"Yes," answered Bea.

I reached for my watch, 7:50. "Bea, we are playing at 2:00. Why are you waking me up now?"

"Yes, you play at 9:00."

"*No*! There is a new schedule. Our game has been changed to 2:00."

"You are not playing?"

"*Yes, I am playing*, but I am playing at 2:00 not 9:00."

"You play two times?"

"*The game has been changed!*" I yelled, nearly cracking my voice box. I just couldn't take it anymore. I hung up the phone and dared her to call me back.

Sleep wouldn't come, so I dressed and went for

breakfast. Through very bleary eyes, I saw Bea enter the restaurant with her head down.

"Toni, sorry. I did not know you play 2:00."

"Yes, you did. I told you. But you wouldn't listen. Why?" I really wanted to know why. Since I had been in Asia, I had been plagued by the question of *Why? Why do they do this stuff?* And it was not a rhetorical question. I really wanted to know what made her do something like this to me. But as usual, I got no answer, only an apology.

"Sorry, sorry, sorry..." she repeated.

"Did you call Christopher and wake him up?"

A blank stare.

"Did you call Christopher and wake him up? Yes or No?"

"No."

"Just me? What am I special?"

No answer.

I handed Bea my cell phone. "Call Christopher, right now, and wake him up."

"But we play two o'clock."

"You woke me up. I want you to wake Christopher up, too."

Maybe I over reacted. But I was just tired of the fact that these people were allowed to screw up any small job they were given, and there would be no negative consequences. If I did stuff like this to the papers I worked for, I'd be unemployed overnight. But Bea could screw up everything, and people would just make up excuses for her.

It was the beginning of an awful day. The one ray of sunshine was that I bumped into Will Hedin in the restaurant. "You were great last night," he said.

I didn't care that I had lost. I had fought. And more importantly, in the end, I had gotten a ton of publicity all over the world. Christopher's press release ran in about thirty media, and journalists from about eight countries covered my event. In some weird way, I suspected that I had lost on purpose, just to prove that I would get more out of my loss than the winner would from his victory. I never knew my opponent's name, and it was never printed in even a single account of the fight. He got a hundred dollars, and nothing more.

The quote, which I gave to the press was *Sometimes charity hurts. Bob Hope wouldn't have to do this, but I can't sing or dance.* It ran right around the globe. I felt guilty because I had mostly stolen it from *Rocky One* and *Rocky Three.*

But Will was the only person who understood my victory.

"Give me your book," he said, meaning the notebook where I did my journalistic writing. I handed it to him, and he quickly wrote, from memory, a wonderful quote from Theodore Roosevelt.

It's not the critic who counts. The credit belongs to the man who is actually in the arena, whose face is marred with dust and sweat and blood. At best, he knows the triumph of high achievement; if he fails, at least he fails while daring greatly, so that his place shall never be with those cold and timid souls who knew neither victory nor defeat.

Once again, Will was dead on. Theodore Roosevelt had been one of my boyhood heroes. Born weak and sickly, he pursued a life of sports, such as swimming and boxing, to build himself up. As an adult he was an adventurer, leading many incredible expeditions, hunting in the American West, and going on safaris in Africa. Eventually, he formed the Rough Riders, an irregular American military unit, which he led, on horseback, into combat in Cuba.

There was no more appropriate man for Will to have recommended to me. And the quote, which I had never read before, was perfect for a boxer. Will had made my day, possibly my week. I later tried to contact him about doing some bush adventure stories together, but he never responded.

Vanessa, one of my journalist friends at the event, had said, "Yes, Will is very interesting. But it is a practiced interesting." She felt that Will might be an ingenuine person, who self-promoted, the same as me. It was a bit of a disappointment, but life goes on.

I asked the hotel desk to call the Kuoni van so I could go to town and use the Internet. I had decided to use this downtime to file some stories – and get paid.

"You can use Internet in the hotel," the girl told me.

I knew about this, but there were two problems. One, it was the slowest, worst Internet service in the world. And second, it cost a whopping US$10 per hour! I had arranged with Rachel to get free Internet cards. But they were an unheard of accommodation, not given to any other journalists. When Phil found out about the free cards, he had a fit. Each card was only good for a half-hour. If I wanted to write for four hours, I didn't feel like asking for a new card eight times. It was better to just go to town and pay US$0.70 per hour.

"No, I want to go to town," I repeated. "Please call the Kuoni van."

"Have van to shopping mall 2:00 PM."

"No, I don't wish to go to the shopping mall. I wish to go to the Internet café. Please call the Kuoni van." I have to add here that I was wearing my Kuoni uniform and name badge.

"Yes, you can take taxi only 300 baht."

"Yes, I could taxi. I agree with you. But I don't want a taxi. I want my van." I didn't want to sound like one of those pampered rock stars, who gets hostile when he hears they have bought the wrong brand of whisky for the bar in the back of his limo. But for an entire week, we had been using our team van, as was customary. Why was it suddenly a problem?

The employee called a manager, and they discussed a long time, in Thai. Then the manager asked, "What would you like?"

A Westerner's assumption would be that the long discussion in Thai would be the employee telling the manager the story. *This guy is from Kuoni. He wants the Kuoni van. But I said* No. But in Asia, you were always starting from zero. Every new person that came over would, ostensibly, know nothing that had already happened. So, the question in my mind is, what exactly is that long discussion about?

"I am on the Kuoni team, and I want our van," I repeated.

"You could take taxi."

She said more. But I had tuned her out. Luckily, at that point a nineteen year-old hotel intern from Sweden walked by.

"Could you please call the Kuoni van?" I asked.

"Certainly," she said, picking up the phone. "They'll be out front in about three minutes," she informed me.

I looked at the other two employees, for any signs of remorse, or that feeling of, *Oh, that's what you wanted. I feel like such an idiot.* But there was no such look. They just smiled.

It didn't matter if it was Thailand or Cambodia. I was at a point that I was going to need a break from Asia soon, or I would explode.

In spite of a far away, buzzing in my hazy head, I managed to file my story and get to the grounds in time for our match.

Paula was there, in rare form, claiming that we owed her money again. She was supposed to have come to the hotel this morning and dropped off photo disks from the fight the night before, so I could give them to Juanita, the press director for the hotel. Juanita would then send them, along with a brilliant press release, to hundreds of media in Thailand and abroad.

When I called Paula during breakfast, she said that the photographer hadn't brought the disk, but she would bring it to us at the polo grounds.

When Paula arrived, she didn't even mention the photos. I was the one who had to bring up the subject.

"I told the photographer to bring them to my house, but he didn't," was all she said, and ordered more free liquor.

At the end of the day, Paula's only contribution to the weeklong event was that she managed to get a professional photographer to cover my fight. And in theory, this was the reason why we allowed her to come to all the events. But if I couldn't get the photos and file them, they were useless to me. Her words were like more blows on my tortured skull.

"Antonio, it's no big deal. You come by my house tonight and get them."

By your house? Tonight? "When tonight? We go from here straight to a huge dinner?"

"OK, I will have him drop them at my house, and send them with a messenger to the hotel. You need to relax more."

This was easy for her to say. She hadn't fought a tough fight the night before. And every minute that I failed to give the photos to Juanita increased the probability that the story would never run. Press releases need to be submitted no later than 5:30 AM the morning after an event, so that they could either make the morning papers of that day, or the next day. If she gave them to me tonight, they wouldn't reach the press till mid-day, the next day, and then the earliest they could run would be on Sunday, four days after the event took place. It was already unlikely that that would happen.

"Cheer up, it's not the end of the world," she said, in a very condescending tone. Next, she brought up the subject of money again. "I heard Jeff is getting US$200 per day. Why aren't you and Christopher paying me that much?"

Because you're not a photographer? was my first thought. Or, *Jeff is paid that much because he has a job, and you don't.* Finally, I went with, "Jeff isn't paid that by the other journalists here. Our agreement was that you were to have a professional photographer out here every day. We would help you get into events, and you would share your photos with us. But so far, you haven't done that. And you've gotten into every single event, all week, for free."

Paula looked angry and hurt. "I don't know what you're implying."

That you're a freeloader, and a bitter alcoholic, who eases her loneliness by pretending to be a journalist.

"But I have tried to get photographers out here. Is it my fault if they don't show up?" she asked, sounding like an innocent, hurt child.

I was going to point out that the spirit of our agreement was that she was responsible for producing professional quality images for us. And since she hadn't done that, she was in violation. Even if I managed to get my boxing photos at this point, they could easily be useless to me. So, once again, she hadn't done what was promised. I was going to explain this to her. But like in the Einarr situation, we were coming from such different places, there was no way she would have seen my point.

I would have been happy to just lay down and die, but Paula continued her ranting.

"Do you know how much I have spent on taxis, running out here every day?"

I didn't. But, I also didn't care. I had never asked her to run out to the polo grounds every day. If she didn't have a professional photographer with her, there was no need for her to come at all.

I went and hid in the coffee tent.

During our worst match up of the week, Christopher called to me from the back half and suggested that Einarr and I switch places, so that he could be where the action was. I immediately agreed, and called a time out. I began riding to Einarr's position, and just as a courtesy said to him, "I think it's better if we switch places, because you are a better player, and we could use you here in the middle."

"Not unless we switch elephants," aid Einarr, defiantly standing his ground. The fact that he would disagree hadn't even entered my mind. Now in addition to the fact that I felt like crap, we had the whole world staring at us, while we bickered.

"There is no time for that," I said. Switching elephants would have entailed riding back to the mounting house, probably costing us half an hour. That would have left the other four players, the referee, and the fans sitting idly in the sun.

"Just switch places with me," I insisted.

"Not unless we change elephants," he repeated. "Yours is faster."

I raised my voice, hoping he would respond to my authority. "Einarr! Everyone is watching. Christopher thinks it's a good idea to switch. I think it's a good idea. Just switch. If we lose because I gave you the wrong elephant, then just blame it on me." I was still riding towards him with the assumption that he would be willing to switch.

"*No*! You have the faster elephant. So, you're stuck playing right where you are," he shouted, sounding like a spoiled little boy in a sailor suit. If he hadn't been sitting on an elephant, he would have stamped his foot.

I couldn't believe it. Was he two years old? What kind of idiot would argue a point this inconsequential? We were losing badly. It was apparent that I was useless where I was. With him there, we had some chance at maintaining our pride. But he was being a Dutch prick about it.

"Is there a problem?" asked the referee.

People were beginning to get impatient.

"No," I said, heading back to my position. "No problem."

"Maybe you and Einarr should switch places," said the referee.

"Einarr, trade with me. The referee even said so." I tried this new line of reasoning.

"No, not unless we switch elephants."

I threw up my hands, in defeat, and rode back to my position.

Now the referee suspected that I was holding on to my position against his recommendations. "Antonio, I really think it would be better for your team if you let Einarr play center."

"I agree. And so does Christopher. But Einarr is refusing to comply."

"Who is team captain?" asked the referee.

"Christopher."

"So why doesn't he tell Einarr to change?"

"Because Einarr is an asshole," I said.

After a twenty-minute delay, we resumed playing, and, as predicted, we lost big. It was our worst defeat. And I vowed I would never play again. As soon as we got off the elephants, I asked Einarr to walk out back with me. I was uncertain if I was going to hit him, or just yell at him. I tried yelling.

"If you ever give me another order, or tell me what to do, I will kill you." Once again I thought my work here was done. It was clear what I had to say. Only an idiot wouldn't see it. I started to walk away.

"What do you mean?" he asked, clueless.

"I mean you made me look like a mook out there today, when you wouldn't switch. Everyone thought it was a good idea. But you wouldn't do it. Even if it was the worst idea in the world, you should have said *Yes*, just to minimize our embarrassment."

"Well, you have to admit it was an illogical idea to have us switch."

I don't have to admit anything. I realized that no amount of talking was going to convince him that he was an idiot. At the same time, if I hit him, I thought he would just get confused. He would have no idea why I was doing it. So I just walked away.

After what had easily been the least enjoyable round of elephant polo a human being ever endured, I tried to get back to the hotel. It was so hot. I was annoyed. And I was coming off a temporary knockout effect from the fight, the night before. It amazed me that I was still on my feet at all.

All I wanted out of life was to take a shower, take a Valium, and sleep for a hundred hours. But when I asked the Kuoni driver to take me back to the hotel he refused.

"What do you mean *No*?" I shouted.

"Other player has to go to hotel," he told me. "Wait for other player."

I assumed that he meant Christopher and Einarr. So I told him it was OK and that we should just go. But he refused again. I looked around for a polo mallet to straighten this misunderstanding out, when it occurred to me, perhaps he meant Robert Stockton. So, I asked him, "Do you mean Robert wants to go back?"

He said, "Yes."

But I knew he was lying. In my dazed state I had forgotten two important facts about Thais. One is that if you say a name, without the prefix of Mister or Miss, they have no idea that you are saying a name. And they have no idea what you are talking about. Once, I had been calling for my friend, Darren, in the guest house which he owned. I asked the employees, "Where is Darren?" They made me repeat it one hundred times, and then told me that they didn't know what I was talking about. I thought, how could they work here and not know the boss' name? But then I remembered, and I asked for Mr.Darren. And they said, "Oh, just one minute. I will go get him."

Fact two was that by proposing a logical, or let's say *acceptable*, reason why we couldn't go, "Richard wants to use the van," the driver now had an "out." All he had to do was agree. And then he would be justified in not taking the van back. And so, that is exactly what he did.

I moped back to the tent, ordered a coffee the way I liked it, set it down on the table, and was accosted by Paula.

"The only money I have seen from any of you is the two hundred baht that Einarr gave me yesterday."

I was trying to tune her out, but this two hundred baht intrigued me.

"Why did you give Paula money?" I asked Einarr, right on front of Paula. I was ready to kill him as it was. But giving her any money at all was just encouragement for her to continue her unacceptable, pestering-us-for-money behavior.

"For my photos, of course," interrupted Paula. "But that is an insult. Some of these photographers get hundreds of dollar per image."

Yes, but they are photographers.

"Why did you buy images from Paula?" I asked. This was a serious breech of our friendship and cooperation. Originally, Paula was giving images to me, only. Christopher asked if he could share images, and I said that it was fine with me if Paula agreed. But this could potentially cause problems, as Christopher and I both published in Chiang Mai. But Einarr wasn't even a journalist. Why was he buying images?

"Well, you know, for stories," he said, lamely.

"What stories? You shouldn't be publishing these images."

"They are my images," said Paula, "and none of you have paid for them."

"If you were going to give Paula money, why didn't you tell us about it?"

There was no answer. What could he say? That he hadn't told us because he was a deceitful person?

A few minutes later, I saw Einarr carrying a suitcase. Apparently, he had decided to head back to Bangkok early. Although I wasn't sad to see Einarr go, I still thought it a bit classless of him not to bother to say goodbye to anyone. I was also annoyed to see him in the Team Kuoni van.

"Oh sure, I can't go back to the hotel, but they will take Einarr to the bus station," I complained.

"Do you want to stop them?" asked Christopher.

"No, I guess not."

By the time the van returned, I was in so much pain that I was curled up in a fetal position on the floor.

"Christopher, please convince them to take me back to the hotel, before I die," I begged.

Christopher sweet-talked Bea, but there was the same communication barrier as before.

"Toni go hotel?" she asked.

"Yes," said Christopher.

"Christopher go hotel also?"

"No, I'd rather like to stay here and see the game."

Bea looked confused. In fact, it had been so long since I had seen her look otherwise that I would have had trouble recognizing her.

"Toni not go hotel?" she asked.

"Yes, Toni go hotel. Christopher stay here watch polo," said Christopher, sounding like Johnny Weismuller.

"Two person go hotel?" asked Bea.

Once again, Christopher showed himself to be a prince among men. "Yes, Toni *and* Christopher go hotel."

We all loaded in the van. The second we drove out the gates of the polo grounds, Christopher said, "Bea, I've changed my mind. I think I would like to stay and watch the game."

Bea looked very nervous. "Toni, no go hotel?"

"Yes, Toni go hotel. Christopher stay here."

"Here?"

"Yes, watch the polo."

"Polo?" she said it as if it were the first time she had heard the word.

"Just slow down," commanded Christopher, in a stern, but not unfriendly voice.

At a traffic light, Christopher jumped out the door

and ran back to the polo grounds.

"Where Christopher go?" asked Bea.

"He's going back to the polo grounds," I answered.

"We go back to polo?"

"*No! We go hotel!*"

"And Christopher?"

Just shut up!

"Christopher will meet us there," I lied.

It was pleasant spending the day with Bea. After the game, Christopher caught a ride with team Mercedes. When I complained about Bea, he said, "It all worked out in the end, didn't it?"

"If you call lying to Bea to get out of the polo grounds, and you running back three kilometers in the heat an acceptable solution, then, yes, it all worked out in the end."

"She probably only earns like a hundred dollars a month," explained Christopher.

"She's only worth half of that."

It had been a hard day for me. And the one thing I had been looking forward to was the five-star dinner that was planned for all the players. It started off well, with a Brazilian-themed cocktail party on the lawn. It wasn't particularly Brazilian, as most of the Thai staff had never heard of Brazil. But there was free booze, and all the freshly cut sushi you could eat. I drank only moderately, but loaded up on uncooked salmon.

There was a brief speech, by a Lord someone or another. The microphone malfunctioned. So, we could only see his lips moving. Luckily, Christopher filled in and narrated for him. "Welcome to the annual elephant polo tournament. I am so wealthy that everyone should envy me. I am quite smashed. I've got my Chivas Regal, my Khmer boys, and I am going to vomit in the swimming pool. This is my lovely wife. She is a charmer. I pay her by the hour."

Next, we were ushered into a tremendous garden, where tables had been laid for the two hundred of us. The first annoyance came when none of the Thai staff could find my table. My invitation said table 26. One would think that it would have been somewhere near table 25. But it wasn't. I asked a staff member to help me. He said "Yes", then walked away and never came back. Two more staff did the same thing. The fourth staff member took me to ten other tables, and tried to convince me that they were all table twenty-six, although the table number was clearly marked, and none of them said twenty-six. Once again, I wondered what would become of these people who couldn't do something as simple as match the number twenty-six, on a card, with the number twenty-six, on a table.

Two seconds after I found my seat, Paula showed up. "Tell them I am Jeff's date," she said, meaning the big photographer who swore he didn't know her.

She was the last person I wanted to see, and they sat her right next to me.

Because of the configuration of the tables, it was only possible to talk to the person on your immediate right or left. I was stuck between Paula and Christopher. But Christopher had already disappeared, leaving me no one to talk to. Being alone and depressed, I turned to drink. But when a waiter informed me that I had to pay cash for my drinks, I gave up on dinner and went to the business center to work on my latest articles. When my free Internet access card ran out, the thought of going back to my room, alone, was too depressing. On a hunch, I stopped by Christopher's room, and found that he had also snuck away from the party.

"We had to pay for drinks. Then Paula showed up, and I thought what's the point?" explained Christopher, mimicking my own feeling on the situation.

It amazed me that Paula was still clueless to the fact that she was unwanted. She had to lie to get into these parties. Then she drove us away...what didn't she see?

Trying to forget Paula, we switched to the other clueless person.

"I asked Einarr why he was leaving," I began. "He said, 'If I don't get back to Chiang Mai soon, I will have too much work to do at the office next week.' But he's an intern! What work could he possibly have to do?"

Christopher laughed. "I'll tell you why he left. It was two things," began Christopher. "One, he has insulted everyone to the point that even he knows he isn't wanted here any longer."

Einarr and Phil had had a child's spat at breakfast, related to the polo shirt that Einarr had loaned him. It was a silly argument, and there no was no reason for it to have become such an issue. One could say that Einarr were right. Phil wasn't really on the team. So, why should he get to keep the jersey? On the other hand, we each had two jerseys. And it obviously meant a lot to Phil. Einarr could have just been gracious and let him keep it. By the end of the too-long argument, Phil hated Einarr.

On a jersey note, Paula had asked me for a jersey. And using the same logic, I would have given her my extra one, but I had already decided to send it back to my editor, Hardy, in Chiang Mai, to thank him for all of his help. But, I did manage to steal her a pith helmet, for which she seemed genuinely excited.

"My second theory on why Einarr left early," continued Christopher, "is that he wants to go to Bangkok, and have sex for money."

"Does he need money that bad?" I asked.

"*No*! I mean he will be *paying* for sex. And he didn't want to say that."

"But this is Thailand. He could just admit that second one, and no one would think anything of it. Besides, he could pay for sex in Chiang Mai. In fact, sometimes, if you use a large bill to pay for a small purchase in a shop, they just offer you sex instead of change."

"I know but this is how he is," commented Christopher. "Personally I think it is a little deviant."

"I saw that you two had words on the field today. How did that go?" he asked.

"To quote Austin Powers, *There are only two things that I hate: people who are intolerant of other people's cultures, and the Dutch.*"

"That well?"

"Yea, trying to get Einarr to see my point was like trying to convince Ralph Nader not to run for president again."

"He isn't high on my list of favorite people right now, either," said Christopher. "He wanted to use my computer. I said, 'Ok,' but I just got it working again after a serious crash, and the virus protection software isn't operative yet, so I told him to go easy. He agreed, but then he stayed logged in for eighteen hours, at a cost of six hundred baht per hour, using the hotel landline, and downloaded porn all day. I checked to see which sites he had been on. There was the Asses Are Bottoms site; and Breasts-A-Million; and Young, Juicy, And Cheap, among others. Now my computer is completely plagued by worms, viruses, Spyware, and who knows what else. It will take months to get it straightened out again. And what does Einarr say when I tell him about it? He said it was my fault. He said that in Holland they would never operate a computer which wasn't virus protected." He shook his head. "*My* fault!"

"Denmark," I corrected.

"You see he's got me so crazy now, I'm doing it

too."

"So, I take it things have been a bit strained between you two." I said, tentatively.

"A little. I mean, he isn't even a journalist. He is an intern. He should be grateful just to even be included on this trip, and now he wants equal shares of everything."

"There is a lot of that going on," I said, meaning Paula.

"That's another subject. But at least I don't have to live with Paula. This morning Einarr comes in here, opens his suitcase, and takes out this huge blanket he brought from the Faro Island, made of whale blubber. He stripped completely naked, rolled up in the blanket, and sucked his thumb for a while. Then he masturbated and released his sphincter. When he finished, he asked me if he could borrow a cigarette."

"The nerve! Cigarettes are expensive."

"You see my point then."

Once we were done griping, we did some work. Christopher wrote the brilliant press release about my fight. Einarr had written one entitled, "Antonio Graecffo loses fight in Huahin." He was obviously missing the point, that we were using this for self-promotion. We didn't have to lie about the outcome of the fight, but it had to be interesting and entertaining, and make people want to buy my books and hire me to write for their magazines.

Christopher's story was called "Writer in the Ring." I knew he was on to something when he asked me, "How much do elephants weigh?"

"I have no idea, like three tons or maybe ten. Why?"

"You'll see," he smirked.

His article was hilarious, and it was one of the single most reprinted articles I had ever been connected with.

Writer in the Ring
By Christopher Atkins

Having spent all week strapped on the back of a three-ton elephant, competing in Huahin's King's Cup elephant polo tournament, American writer Antonio Graceffo stepped away from the paddock to take part in an exhibition boxing match in the seaside town's Grand Sports Stadium to raise awareness for the elephant's cause.

The King's Cup tournament, now in its fourth year, was competed by fourteen teams drawn from around the globe to raise money for the Lampang Elephant Conservation Center (LECC) in Northern Thailand. With the initial forecast of raising 1.5 million baht for the project looking likely to be exceeded, and a fantastic week's entertainment had by all involved, the tournament has been a resounding success.

Graceffo, who boxes part-time and has even starred in a recent Cambodian kung fu flick, strapped on his gloves in front of a packed crowd and gave a rousing performance. In a closely fought three-round contest, Antonio was unlucky to come out on the wrong side of a tight decision, but was happy to have accomplished his mission of letting people know about the ECC's work.

"Sometimes charity hurts," laughed Graceffo. "If I were Bob Hope, I wouldn't have to do this – but I can't sing or dance."

The next morning, though, it was back to the elephant polo ground to try and help his team of fellow journalists, sponsored by UK travel agency Kuoni, get through the next round.

With our work out of the way, we settled down, Christopher on one bed, me on the other. We channel surfed, and talked until the wee hours. The unspoken sentiment was that we were really glad to have met and to have worked together.

Christopher told me about when he had been an exchange student in Germany, and how he regretted that he had pissed his great learning experience away, drinking and behaving ladishly, rather than cracking the books and mastering the language.

"I stayed out till the pub closed one night and missed the last train back. So, I had to call my host family for a pick up." He dialed the number, his first phone call in Germany, but when his host-mother picked up, she sounded drunk. In his elementary German, he told her. "This is Christopher. I missed the train. Could you please come get me?" But the host mother replied, "What? What? I don't know what you are saying. Please never call here again." And she slammed down the phone.

"I was only fourteen," said Christopher, obviously reliving what had been a painful memory. "I'd never been abroad before. The only thing I could do was call again." This time, when she picked up, he said, "Hello, this is Christopher."

"Who?" she replied.

"The English boy. I missed the train; please come get me."

But she screamed into the phone, "Stop calling me!!!"

Christopher looked around for anyone who could help him. It was a small village, without a lot of people to begin with. But once the pubs closed, the streets were deserted. Next, it began to rain, making the experience even more pleasant. Finally, a policeman happened along, and Christopher asked him for help.

"When I realized what had gone wrong, I could have shot myself," said Christopher.

The policeman explained to Christopher, that when he was making a local call from inside of Germany, he had to eliminate the first several digits of the phone number. It turned out that he had been calling Switzerland.

"This poor, old woman sitting in a chocolate chair, under a cuckoo clock, and wearing a very expensive watch, suddenly received these panicked phone calls from Britain's lost youth," laughed Christopher. "I could imagine how upset she was."

I am not sure how Christopher and I got on the subject of sex. Well, we were guys with nothing to do. So I guess that is common ground, especially since I don't like football.

"I've had a threesome with two girls," bragged Christopher.

"Did you pay for it?"

"Yes."

"Anyone could do that," I pointed out, knocking down the greatest achievement of his life.

"Oh yeah! Well anyone could rock climb up a waterfall, the wrong way," he said. Obviously, he had read one of my river-tracing adventure stories on-line. "But not everyone does it, now do they?"

He had a point.

The next morning, we played our final game, against St. Regis team.

≡249

"They invented the game," said Christopher

"Yea, I heard they were pretty good," I seconded.

"No, I mean they *invented* the game. They are the original team of Sir Niles and his lorded friends."

It was a complete slaughter. Not only did we lose, but one of the players hit me in the head with his mallet and didn't even apologize. My first instinct was to hit him back. But I figured that he could use a mallet better than me, and I would get creamed. Now I cursed Christopher for not letting me bring my grappling hook and boarding-cutlass as I had originally wanted to.

"We could swing across on ropes, and force the other players to walk the plank," I had suggested. But Christopher had some crazy idea that this would have been a breech of etiquette.

"After all, we are guests at this function," he had said.

As the whole polo tournament had had a distinctly British feel to it, I tended to defer to Christopher on matters of polite behavior. But now, I was sorry that I was unarmed.

I also couldn't help seeing the irony in the fact that this entirely British, and exceptionally lavish, occasion was financed by an American. For me, elephant polo was an allegory for twentieth century world history. A further analogy would be, the polite British gentleman would get away with cracking me in the skull with his mallet, because I was too poor to play polo on my own and should learn to accept the abuse that came with the *haves* making room for us *have nots* at their table.

British lords unfairly repressing the masses... Didn't we fight a war over that once?

The day was incredibly hot. I was exhausted by nearly a week of tournament life. I hated sports with a passion, and the weirdness of the game had worn off days earlier. Einarr was gone, but he had worn me down, always telling me what to do.

"Antonio, you really need to take the game more seriously."

You really need to take the life more lightly, I wanted to say.

But he was in Bangkok, having sex for money. If he had been there on that final day, I would have pulverized him. The second they handed me that two-and-a-half meter-long mallet, his life would have been in danger. The population sign on the Faro Islands would have to be changed from 40,000 to 39,999.

I was tired of Phil and Paula worming their way deeper and deeper into the tournament. Already Phil wanted to know why Robert Stockton had a private jet, and he didn't. Paula wanted to know why she wasn't invited to play in the tournament. When she saw the loving cup that the winning team would be awarded, she got particularly jealous and demanded that someone give her one. Christopher compromised by giving her a cup of Chivas, and she quieted down. But she was still bitching about money.

"I haven't seen dollar one from you three!" she complained.

I wasn't sure why she expected to see any money from us. We never promised any. And this was coming from a woman who had received a free five-star meal every day for the last week, simply because she claimed to be with us.

An upshot was that I received an e-mail from a friend saying that my book *The Monk from Brooklyn,* about my experiences at the Shaolin Temple, had finally been released. He had just ordered a copy from Amazon.com

We had lost all of our matches and placed fourteenth in the tournament – of fourteen. But in the World League of Elephant Polo, there are only about twenty teams, so that's not that bad.

"We are the worst," Einarr had complained, seeing our results posted on the big board before he had left.

At breakfast on the final morning, most of the other teams consoled us about being in 14th place.

"There are five-and-a-half billion people in the world," I pointed out. "And out of that number, only about thirty-five can beat us at elephant polo. That sounds good to me. There is no need to eat humble pie."

"Did someone say something about free food?" asked Christopher.

Christopher and I gorged ourselves on the last free buffet we would get out of the tournament, and then charged a bottle of Chivas, using a tracing of one of Einarr's credit card receipts which we found in the trash.

"Where are your bags?" I asked Christopher, as my own kit was packed and ready.

"We don't have to be out of the rooms till three," He said, hoping to milk the experience for all that it was worth.

Originally, I was told that I would be taking public transport back to Bangkok, but Phil arranged for me to ride back with him in the limo. He was going to be covering the food and wine show at one of Robert Stockton's other hotels in Bangkok.

While this may have been a last hurrah for small time journalists, like Christopher and me, people like Phil lived like this all the time.

Christopher and I toasted the elephants, toasted free English education for Thais, and toasted freeloaders. When the limo driver became impatient, Christopher and I had a final drink; we raised our glasses and drank to the thing which defined our entire week together.

To the Dutch!

About the Author

Antonio Graceffo, BA, Dip Lic, AAMS, CMFC, CTC, RFC

Born to Italian parents, Antonio is originally from New York City. He spent seven years in the United States Military, in both the Army NG and the US Merchant Marines. Antonio is fluent in German, Spanish, Italian, and Mandarin Chinese, and speaks Thai and Khmer conversationally. He holds diplomas from Tennessee State University; University of Mainz, Germany; Trinity College, England; Heriot Watt University, Scotland; Universidad Latina, Costa Rica – as well as advanced degrees in business and taxation from various universities in the United States.

Antonio has studied and competed in martial arts and boxing for over twenty-five years and has studied at the Shaolin Temple, in Mainland China, and at a Muay Thai (boxing) temple, in Thailand. He works as a full time adventurer, writer, and film star.

He currently lives in Cambodia, where he is staring in Kung Fu films and boxing professionally.

Antonio's writings have appeared in the following publications: *Bangkok Post, Farang, Escape Artist, Travel in Taiwan, Taiwan Ho, Travelmag* (UK), *Good Morning Chiang Mai, Travellers Impressions, The Chiang Mai Mail, Marco Polo, The Huahin Observer, Centered on Taipei, The Pattaya Trader, Life Style Taiwan, Canoe* (Canada), *Views Unplugged, Kung Fu Magazine, The Little Magazine, Yellow Times,* Bike China, *Small Boat Forum, Holiday Times*

(Thailand), *Writing World, All Things Global, The Write Market, The Rose and Thorn, Blueberry Press, The Elizabethton Star, Go Nomad, Close Quarters Combat, Hack Writers, Go World, Bike League of America, Martial Arts Planet, The Travel Rag, Black Belt Magazine, The Bristol Herald Courier, Radical Adventures, The Investment Advisor, I Soldi, America Oggi, The Italian Tribune, Pagina Uno, The Italian Voice, Tales of Asia, Buddha Fist, Canoe* (CA), *Khmer Connection, Angkor, The Cambodian Scene, The Phnom Penh Post, The Cambodia Daily, Intradevi, Off Beat Travel, Khmer Youth, Crossbow Hunter, Cambodian Web, Jade Dragon, Blue Lotus Club, Double Standard, Independent Media, Kampuchea,* acres.org.sg., *Primo Magazine.*

Antonio's travel writing was featured in an anthology, published in the UK, entitled *Travellers Tales from Heaven and Hell Part Two.*

Antonio's book about his studies at the Shaolin Temple, *The Monk from Brooklyn,* has been published by Gom Publishing and is available at amazon.com, barnesandnoble.com, and gompublishing.com.

His book, *Boats, Bikes, & Boxing Gloves: An adventure writer in the Kingdom of Siam* is also available at amazon.com, barnesandnoble.com, and gompublishing.com.

Film Credits

Antonio co-starred in the Khmer Kung Fu film *Krabei Liak Goan* (Buffalo Protecting Child)

Contact the author at: antonio_graceffo@hotmail.com

9 781932 966374